Joint Commission
RESOURCES

D1791581

ASSESSING
HOSPITAL STAFF
COMPETENCE

Joint Commission Resources Mission

The mission of Joint Commission Resources is to continuously improve the safety and quality of care in the United States and in the international community through the provision of education and consultation services and international accreditation.

Joint Commission Resources educational programs and publications support, but are separate from, the accreditation activities of the Joint Commission. Attendees at Joint Commission Resources educational programs and purchasers of Joint Commission Resources publications receive no special consideration or treatment in, or confidential information about, the accreditation process.

Printed in the U.S.A. 5 4 3 2 1
Requests for permission to reprint or make copies of any part of this book should be addressed to:
Permissions Editor
Joint Commission Resources
One Renaissance Boulevard
Oakbrook Terrace, IL 60181

ISBN: 0-86688-735-0
Library of Congress Catalog Number: 2002108808

For more information about Joint Commission Resources, please visit our Web site at *www.jcrinc.com*. For more information about the Joint Commission on Accreditation of Healthcare Organizations, please visit *www.jcaho.org*.

Table of Contents

Chapter 4. Initial Competence Assessment of Licensed Independent Practitioners

93

Chapter 5. Continuing Competence Assessment of Licensed Independent Practitioners

127

Selected Readings

147

Index

149

Introduction

Ensuring the competence of individuals who work in all hospital areas is key to a hospital's ability to meet the needs of patients as defined in its mission. In addition, ensuring the competence of individuals working in and for the hospital is essential to achieving quality patient care outcomes and patient safety. How can hospitals achieve these ends? Through complete and timely competence assessment—a process that entails using performance appraisal, credentials review, and privileging activities to evaluate and verify a person's capability of meeting job expectations. Hospital leaders must ensure that the competence of everyone working in or for the organization is assessed. This applies whether the employee provides direct care or not; whether he or she is employed directly by the hospital or by an entity with whom the hospital has contracted; or whether he or she is an employee, independent contractor, licensed independent practitioner (LIP), volunteer, student, or temporary worker.

Assessing Hospital Staff Competence offers practical, effective strategies for assessing competence in hospitals. It covers assessing the competence of individuals covered by Joint Commission Human Resources standards as well as LIPs covered by the Medical Staff standards. Developed for human resource leaders and staff, medical staff directors

and coordinators, and performance improvement staff, the book addresses competence assessment issues specific to each type of professional. Forms, examples, and policies and procedures illustrate how the competence assessment process can be applied to the many types of workers who perform tasks for hospitals.

Compliance with Joint Commission competence assessment standards has been problematic for many hospitals in recent years. This book was developed to address the need for additional information in this area. It provides in-depth explanations of each competence assessment standard, examples of how to best comply with the standard, information on common compliance problems, and tips for improving the competence assessment process. Separate sections address individuals covered by the Human Resources standards (non-LIPs) and those covered by the Medical Staff standards (LIPs). To minimize interruptions to the flow of the text, lengthy examples are included at the end of each chapter.

Overview of Contents

Chapter 1 defines the terms and concepts used throughout the book, including competence, competence assessment, competencies for special patient populations, cultural competence, LIP, allied health professional, credentialing, and privileging. It also provides an overview of the essential elements of a successful competence assessment program. The goal of Chapter 1 is to establish a common understanding of issues related to competence.

Chapter 2 covers initial competence assessment of individuals covered by the Human Resources standards. It outlines JCAHO requirements and describes how hospitals define competencies—including general, department-specific, job-specific, population-specific, and cultural and linguistic competencies. It also covers how hospitals assess an individual's abilities during the interview process, during orientation, and upon completion of the orientation process. Examples of compliance, information on how surveyors measure adherence to the requirements, common problem areas, and improvement tips are provided.

Chapter 3 covers the topic of continuing competence assessment and maintenance of LIPs covered by the Human Resources standards. Following a description of JCAHO requirements, the chapter describes how hospitals lay the groundwork of an ongoing competence assessment process. This involves identifying competencies, establishing the frequency of assessment, determining who assesses competence and the methods used, and other key activities. The chapter then describes competence assessment methods, including observation, demonstrations of skill, written tests and documentation, the role of education and training, and the use of data to identify and address staff learning needs. Examples of compliance, information on how surveyors measure adherence to the requirements, common problem areas, and improvement tips are provided.

Chapter 4 covers how hospitals ensure the initial competence of LIPs covered by the Medical Staff standards. It describes how hospitals define the scope of privileges to be offered by the organization and various privilege classification systems. The chapter also addresses how the current competence of LIPs is assessed through the credential review and privileging process, which culminates in a decision on hospital medical staff appointment and the granting of clinical privileges. The importance of delineating clinical privileges and the role of proctoring also are described. The chapter includes examples of compliance, information on how surveyors measure adherence to the requirements, common problem areas, and improvement tips.

Chapter 5 covers continuing competence assessment of LIPs covered by the Medical Staff standards. It describes how assurance of the ongoing competence of practitioners is the goal of the reappraisal, reappointment, and renewal of clinical privileges processes. The chapter includes information related to how the applicant provides evidence of current competence when applying for reappointment or renewal of clinical privileges, and how the medical staff gathers and evaluates competence-related data and makes a decision regarding reappointment and/or the renewal of clinical privileges. Finally, as do other chapters, it concludes with information on what surveyors look for in a hospital's process for assessing the continuing competence of LIPs and common problem areas and improvement tips.

The Selected Readings section guides readers to literature of interest, and the Index enables readers to access information by key word.

Using This Book

The examples, tools, forms, checklists, tips, and documents included in this book come from a range of hospitals. Some of the information may be relevant to your hospital or program; some may not. Staff in each hospital must create competence assessment processes, policies, and documents that are best suited to the organization's specific needs based on its mission and patient population. You are encouraged to use the information included here as a reference and starting point and to adapt it to meet your hospital's specific needs for a comprehensive competence assessment plan.

Acknowledgments

We would like to thank the many organizations that contributed materials to this book. Their contributions have greatly enhanced the publication. A special thanks goes to Denise Woolley, CMSC, CPCS, director, Medical Staff Services, Memorial Hospital, Fremont, Ohio, and Cheryl Eckley, CPCS, UHHS Bedford Medical Center, Bedford, Ohio. We also wish to acknowledge the contribution of the writer of the publication, Nancy Gorham Haiman.

CHAPTER 1

Building the Foundation

Use of the terms and application of the concepts related to competence and competence assessment vary widely from hospital to hospital, from health care professional to health care professional, and in the professional literature. Hospital leaders, therefore, must develop a shared vision of competence, ensure that all individuals who work in the hospital understand the basic terms and concepts, and strive to ensure a consistent application of competence assessment across the organization. A common understanding lays the basic foundation necessary for developing and implementing a cost-effective, high-quality, hospitalwide competence assessment program.

Defining the Terms

What Does Competency Mean?

Competence. Competency. Competent. We may think we know what the words mean, but, in fact, our definitions vary widely. Some use the words synonymously; others suggest that the words are subtly but essentially different. The professional literature is replete with different definitions of the term *competence*. "The word *competence* has gained so much popularity in so many circles that its meaning must be clarified by anyone planning to profess it, measure it, assess it, or develop it," notes Karen J. Kelly-Thomas, author of a nursing staff development

text.[1] Table 1-1, Common Definitions Found in Health Care Literature, on page 2, presents a summary of these definitions.

JCAHO's Definition of Competency

JCAHO uses the words *competence* and *competency* synonymously. According to the glossary in the most recent *Comprehensive Accreditation Manual for Hospitals: The Official Handbook* and the second edition of the *Lexicon: A Dictionary of Health Care Terms, Organizations, and Acronyms*, competence or competency is "a determination of an individual's capability to perform up to defined expectations."[2,3] Other Joint Commission publications give a more detailed definition. In these, competence is defined as the knowledge, skills, ability, and behaviors that a person possesses in order to perform tasks correctly and skillfully. In employment settings, competence is a person's capability of performing job expectations properly, as verified through performance appraisal activities. [4,5]

Competence involves knowledge, skill, and critical thinking. *Knowledge* is the preparation for performance. It is the information needed to meet performance expectations in a given situation. *Skill* is the demonstration of performance—the ability to do something well. Knowledge is assumed to exist by the completion of course work, written tests,

Table 1-1

Summary of Definitions Found in Health Care Literature

Term	Definition
Competence	An individual's capacity to perform his or her job responsibilities.
Competency	An individual's actual performance of his or her specific job responsibilities.
Competence assessment	The process of evaluating an individual's potential knowledge and skills.
Competency assessment	The process of verifying an individual's ability to perform and apply knowledge and skills.
Competencies	A relatively new word, which describes the skills considered by the organization to be necessary to perform a specific job or service.

SOURCE: Adapted from McConnell EA: Competence vs. competency. *Nurs Manage* 32(5): 14, May 2001, and Kelly-Thomas KJ: *Clinical and Nursing Staff Development: Current Competence, Future Focus.* Philadelphia: Lippincott Williams and Wilkins, 1998, p 74.

licensure, and experience. Skill, on the other hand, can be confirmed only by direct observation of an individual's performance or the outcomes of that performance. Knowledge doesn't necessarily result in skill, but skill is evidence of knowledge.

According to the *Oxford American Dictionary*, a person is competent when he or she is properly qualified or skilled. Used as an adjective in the hospital setting, the word *competent* thus describes a person who has demonstrated the ability to perform adequately the specific skill or skills defined by the hospital as important. The person has achieved a practice level that is consistent with his or her practice goals as defined by the organization. The word *incompetent*—or, preferably, *not competent*—by contrast, is often used to describe a person who is not qualified or able to perform a particular task or function and is not performing up to the standards defined by the organization.

Competence involves at least three different types of skill categories—cognitive, psychomotor, and interpersonal skills, as outlined in Sidebar 1-1,

Components of Competence, page 3. Typically, for example, hospital managers develop job or position descriptions that state both the qualifications needed to get the job and the specific knowledge, cognitive, psychomotor, and interpersonal skills necessary to perform it competently. The delineation of the clinical privileges process accomplishes this function for licensed independent practitioners, a topic addressed fully in Chapter 4.

Experts' Definitions of Competencies

Writing in a training and development journal, PA McLagan describes competencies as including [6]

- Tasks: the activities and procedures involved in a job;
- Results: the ability to produce a particular result;
- Outputs: the ability to produce, provide, or deliver a certain something;
- Knowledge, skills, and attitudes: the subject matter, process abilities, and attitudes, values, orientations, and commitments involved in doing a job; and

- Attribute bundles: a collection of knowledge, skills, and attitudes or tasks, outputs, and results, such as leadership, problem solving and decision making.

Others outline "competency characteristics" that should be considered, including motives (the things a person consistently thinks about or wants that cause action); traits (physical characteristics and consistent responses to situations or information); self-concept (a person's attitudes, values, or self-image); knowledge (that is, information a person has in specific content areas); and skill (that is, the ability to perform a certain physical or mental task).[7] Still others describe *types* of competency, such as

- Generic: those characteristics required across all jobs, such as decision-making and problem-solving ability, professionalism and accountability, customer service focus, and effective communication;
- Job-specific: competencies related to tasks, such as management or supervision for those who perform those jobs; and
- Threshold: the minimal requirements to hold the job. These are the generic knowledge, license, or skills that are essential to performing a job but are not causally related to superior job performance.[8, 9]

However the term is defined or categorized, individuals acquire and enhance competence through the initial training they receive, orientation provided by the hospital, retraining, on-the-job experience, and continuing education. The relationship among these aspects of the competence continuum is shown in Figure 1-1, The Competency Continuum, page 4.

Competence Assessment

The Joint Commission defines competence assessment or competency assessment as the process of using performance appraisal activities to evaluate and verify a person's capability to perform job expectations properly. This process applies to

---

Sidebar 1-1

Components of Competence

Cognitive, psychomotor, and interpersonal skills are critical to competence and successful job performance. For continued competence, these skills must be assessed, maintained, and improved.

- *Cognitive skills* involve the ability to analyze and "see" the true importance of observations and events. Being able to think critically—to analyze a situation and anticipate future events—enables one to be proactive rather than reactive.
- *Psychomotor skills* involve the ability to perform physical tasks that are learned from books, lectures, videotapes, and skill-based training, such as CPR or insertion of a central-line catheter.
- *Interpersonal skills* involve the ability to work with others. For example, meeting, greeting, and interviewing patients or working effectively within an assigned team involve interpersonal skills. Due to the interdisciplinary nature of health care, staff must be competent in the ability to work with others. Some educators also include interests, attitudes, values, appreciation, and emotions in a broader fourth domain of learning category, called "affective skills."

- all individuals working in and for the hospital, whether providing direct care or not;
- contract or agency personnel;
- volunteers;
- students of all disciplines;
- licensed independent practitioners; and
- allied health professionals.

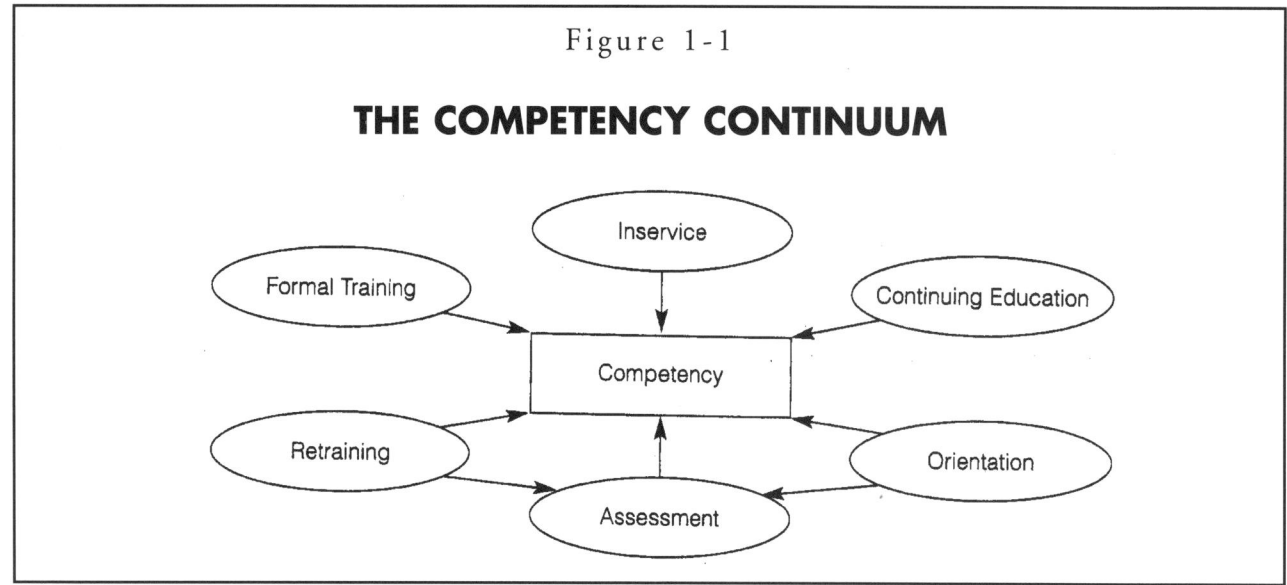

Figure 1-1

THE COMPETENCY CONTINUUM

The interrelationship of the components of competency.
SOURCE: Anne C. Belanger, MA, MT. Originally published in "Practical, ongoing competency-assessment program for hospital pharmacists and technicians," American Society of Health-System Pharmacists, Inc. All rights reserved. Reprinted with permission.

In short, it applies to everyone who works in the hospital setting or to entities operated by the hospital.

Assessing competence occurs over a continuum as an ongoing process. For individuals covered by the Human Resources standards, competence assessment involves the initial and continuing appraisal of an individual's ability to fulfill specific responsibilities or expectations stated in job descriptions. For those covered by the Medical Staff standards, the assessment process focuses initially on verification of current competence and the ability to perform requested privileges and/or assume an appointment to the medical staff. After the individual has been appointed and/or granted privileges, the focus shifts to continual monitoring of the individual's competence through a variety of mechanisms.

A sample competence assessment framework for a nurse's coordination of patient care illustrates the relationship between competence assessment and an individual's progress in acquiring technical, interpersonal, and critical thinking skills. For each competency, the organization defines the skills required in each domain. See Figure 1-2, Registered

Professional Nurse Competency Assessment: Coordination of Patient Care, page 5.

Competencies for Special Patient Populations

Competencies for special patient populations involve the knowledge, skills, ability, and behaviors essential for providing care to specific populations of patients such as neonatal, pediatric, adolescent, and geriatric patients. They include the specific skills and technical knowledge and the more general knowledge related to growth and development over the human life span. Appropriate competence for special patient populations is critical to the provision of quality patient care. Indeed, patients have a right to be assessed, cared for, and educated by competent individuals who are knowledgeable about and sensitive to their special needs.

For example, clinical staff who work with infants must know how to draw blood specimens using micro-techniques. Similarly, patients in the neonatal or pediatric age group are not yet able to understand the treatment that is administered to them;

Figure 1-2

Registered Professional Nurse Competency Assessment: Coordination of Patient Care

	TECHNICAL	INTERPERSONAL	CRITICAL THINKING
NOVICE	Assigns all patients and unit activities on a timely basis.	Communicates changes in medical/nursing orders in timely fashion.	Sees that all assignments are completed for shift.
	Enters orders into EHIS accurately.	Reports objective data to MD, other shift and nurse managers.	Recognizes significant changes in patient status and seeks appropriate resources.
	Completes patient classification report and sends to nursing office each shift.		
	Sees that discharge summary/instructions are done for all potential discharges.		
ADVANCED BEGINNER	Completes patient care assignment based on acuity of needs, job description and level of caregiver skill.	Initiates contacts with other departments to ensure that patient care needs are met.	Begins to evaluate quality of care delivered by others.
	Revises and updates nursing orders as needed.	Communicates with MD and other caregivers, giving complete and accurate information regarding patient condition.	Evaluates change in patient status and reports complete and accurate information to appropriate resource.
	Organizes work load to maximize efficiency.		Delegates activities in routine situations and in some urgent situations.
	Participates and follows up with established plan of care.		
COMPETENT	Accepts responsibility as dictated by unit needs.	Actively initiates effective communication patterns among team members.	Aware of staff weakness and utilizes staff strengths in coordinating patient care.
	Plans for continuity in each patient's care over all shifts and over sustained periods of time (24-hour awareness of patient needs).	Coordinates and cooperates with other care providers for productive problem solving to meet patient needs.	Uses sound clinical judgment when delegating responsibilities during emergency situations.
	Facilitates resourceful use of organization's policies and procedures by all unit members.	Resource for staff members; communicating appropriate knowledge, skills and conduct.	Identifies conflicting medical/nursing orders and takes appropriate action.
	Adapts to changing workloads with flexibility, reprioritizing needs and guiding other staff in adjusting work loads.	Creates a practice environment that maximizes individual performance.	Recognizes opportunities to change patient care delivery or nursing care practices that will improve quality of patient care.

SOURCE: Robinson SM, Barberis-Ryan C: Competency assessment: A systematic approach. *Nurs Manage* 26(2): 40–44, Feb 1995, p 44. Used with permission.

unable to verbalize their responses to treatment, these patients frequently express themselves in non-verbal ways. Thus, staff who assess, treat, or care for neonatal or pediatric patients must be competent at interpreting nonverbal cues.

Adolescent patients pose yet a different challenge because this population frequently resists adult authority. Therefore, to enlist an adolescent in his or her treatment requires understanding that an authoritarian approach is unlikely to succeed.

Geriatric patients have needs commonly related to physical and sensory limitations (such as fragile skin, hearing loss, incontinence, and so on), unique psychosocial needs, and age-associated conditions (such as Alzheimer's disease). Staff members who work with such patients must have the corresponding knowledge and skills to meet these special needs. All staff who have regular clinical contact with patients from these population groups must be competent in providing age-appropriate care.

Cultural and Linguistic Competence

According to the Department of Health and Human Services Office of Minority Health and Resources for Cross Cultural Care, cultural competence involves a set of attitudes, skills, behaviors, and policies that enable an individual to work respectfully and effectively with patients and each other in a culturally diverse work environment. Culture defines the values, beliefs, customs, knowledge, and practices shared by a group and can affect an individual's perception of health care providers, as well as the many types of services related to the provision of care. Culture spans such concepts as race, ethnicity, gender, profession, age, and physical ability. In the delivery of health care services, cultural competence involves sensitivity to and knowledge of the relevance of a patient's cultural background in any component of service delivery, including

• patient education materials;
• questionnaires;
• interviews; and
• bedside manner.

It entails considering a patient's ethnic, regional, religious, and other affiliations when giving care, and involves treating each patient with human dignity and avoiding behavior based on prejudice or stereotype.

Cultural competence reflects the ability to acquire and use knowledge of the health-related beliefs, attitudes, practices, and communication patterns of patients and their families to improve services, strengthen programs, increase community participation, and close the gaps in health status among diverse population groups. It entails an awareness and acceptance of cultural differences; self-awareness; knowledge of the patient's culture; and adaptation of skills. Cultural competence requires a health care professional's understanding and sensitivity to population-specific issues including

• health-related beliefs and cultural values, including beliefs and nutritional preferences (the socioeconomic perspective);
• disease prevalence (the epidemiological perspective); and
• treatment and patient care practices (the outcome perspective).[10, 11]

For example, some Chinese patients believe in the principles of feng shui, which hold that a person's energy flow is affected by the physical environment. This health-related belief has implications for the color, design, and placement of treatment rooms and the patient experience within them. Similarly, cultural competence requires sensitivity to ensuring a quiet space for religious patients who may wish to pray. Knowledge of disease prevalence in specific racial and ethnic groups also is critical. Culturally competent practitioners who treat patients in a community that is populated heavily by southeast Asians, for example, will be aware that Vietnamese women have a higher incidence of cervical cancer than their Caucasian counterparts.[12] Moreover, all culturally competent practitioners will be aware that medication compliance is not uniform across different ethnic groups. Patient care practices, such as the education provided to patients and their families about proper medication compliance, should reflect the current state of knowledge about compliance within diverse ethnic groups.

To acquire cultural competence in health care, individuals must develop and maintain interpersonal and professional skills that increase their respect, understanding, and knowledge of the differences between patient and practitioner in values, lifestyles, norms, beliefs, and opportunities that influence every aspect of the health care delivery system. Although there is no one set of criteria for establishing cultural competence, many interpretations and models can offer a conceptual framework. A key step toward developing cultural competency is heightening self-awareness and analyzing one's values, goals, and prejudices that enter every clinical encounter. Lack of awareness about and sensitivity to cultural differences can make it difficult for both health care team members and patients and their families to achieve the best, most appropriate care.[13] Sidebar 1-2, "Dimensions of Culture" below, identifies the dimensions of culture and related questions that health care workers should consider when rendering care to a patient.

Sidebar 1-2

Dimensions of Culture

Dimension	Questions to Consider
Health and illness beliefs	What paradigm is used to explain illness/healing?
Decision-making style	Does decision making rest with the individual patient, the group/family, or community peers?
Healing traditions	What are the alternative/complementary approaches used for healing? What is the role of traditional healers (eg, shamans)?
Locus of control	Is the individual responsible for his or her own destiny or is destiny predetermined?
Status/hierarchy	Is the status of head of household conferred by age, gender or kinship? What status is attributed to physicians and healers?
Privacy	Is privacy at the level of the individual or the family?
Communication	Is there a preferred mode of communication (eg, spoken, written, sign)? Is there a preferred language (eg, English, Spanish)? Is an interpreter needed? Is a cultural broker needed?
Socioeconomic status	Is social status in the community conferred based on family, vocation, wealth, or education?
Immigrant status	Are the patient/family immigrants? How long have they been living in the U.S.? Are there acculturation and generational issues at play? Is immigrant status a potential legal concern?

SOURCE: Mutha S, Allen C, Welch M: *Toward Culturally Competent Care: A Toolbox for Teaching Communication Strategies.* Center for the Health Professions, the University of California, San Francisco, 2002. Used with permissions.

Whose Competence Is Being Assessed?

Licensed Independent Practitioners

A licensed independent practitioner (LIP) is any individual permitted by law and the hospital to provide care and services, without direction or supervision, within the scope of the individual's license and consistent with individually granted clinical responsibilities.

Physicians are the most obvious example of LIPs. The state grants them a license to provide care and services without direction or supervision, *and* the hospital permits them to provide care and services without direction or supervision. The definition has been applied to dentists, osteopaths, oral and maxillofacial surgeons, and podiatrists. As indicated by this definition, the threshold issue in determining LIP status is the scope of the state license. State laws determine which professions are considered independent, but even these laws might be ambiguous. The scope of practice permitted under a license varies from state to state. According to the Joint Commission standards, hospitals may define the professions that are considered to be LIPs, as long as such definitions conform with state laws. For example, Alaska considers nurse practitioners, by law, to be LIPs. Clinical psychologists, registered dietitians, chiropractors, and clinical social workers also are LIPs in many states. Sidebar 1-3, "Without Direction or Supervision": What Does This Mean? page 9, defines further the phrase "without direction or supervision."

Allied Health Professionals

The Joint Commission defines an allied health professional (AHP) as a health professional qualified by training and frequently by licensure to assist, facilitate, or complement the work of physicians, dentists, podiatrists, nurses, pharmacists, and other specialists in the health care system.

Each hospital, however, uses the designation AHP differently. The term often is defined by example.

Some hospitals, for instance, refer to *allied staff* as including certified registered nurse anesthetists (CRNAs), nurse practitioners, or physician's assistants. Some hospitals may use the term *associates* to describe a dietitian, surgical scrub technician, or office RN. Still others will use *allied health practitioners* to describe all of these individuals. Usually, the medical staff bylaws will define these terms.

One important distinction among AHPs is whether they may practice independently or must work under the supervision of a physician, dentist, or podiatrist. They are categorized as licensed independent practitioners or dependent AHPs, depending on whether they can practice independently. Independent allied health professionals may provide patient care services in or for a hospital *only within the limits* set by the hospital medical staff, while an LIP's degree of patient care is decided upon by policy or privileges that the governing board recommends or approves. Hospitals should be aware of their state's licensure provisions regarding independent practice and state requirements for the supervision of AHPs. Legal counsel can provide advice and clarify any ambiguities.

Examples of potential LIPs, where permitted by law and regulation, include

- advanced nurse practitioners,
- physician assistants;
- psychologists;
- clinical social workers;
- registered dietitians; and
- chiropractors.

Dependent Allied Health Professionals. AHPs who are not licensed and authorized to practice independently by both the state and the hospital are categorized as *dependent* AHPs. Dependent AHPs are licensed, certified, or trained (as applicable by law), to perform patient care services under the supervision of a practitioner who has staff privileges. Dependent AHPs include health professionals who

Sidebar 1-3

"Without Direction or Supervision": What Does This Mean?

Considerable controversy surrounds the phrase "without direction or supervision."

In some states, certain practitioners are permitted to care for patients within the scope of their license only on *referral* from a physician. Some organizations mistakenly interpret this to mean that the practitioner is practicing under supervision. In reality, the only relationship between the practitioner and the physician is the referral; no supervision occurs. In other states, these same practitioners may be able to set up an office and care for patients who come to them directly (for example, clinical social workers, physical therapists, and advanced nurse practitioners).

When physicians provide services using practice guidelines or protocols, they are practicing under direction and supervision to an extent—the direction of the organization that wrote the protocol, and the supervision of the organization that reviews their adherence to the protocol. In most cases, the physician can deviate from the protocol, but that deviation must be scrutinized for appropriateness. The physician maintains independence while following accepted guidelines. When other practitioners (for example, clinical social workers or physicians' assistants) use practice guidelines or protocols, the line between working independently and working under supervision begins to blur.

Hospitals have the authority and responsibility to determine which professions will be granted clinical responsibilities for identified patient care services, in accordance with law and regulations.

are licensed by the state to practice independently but are limited by the hospital to practicing under supervision. For example, the state licensing laws may permit CRNAs to practice independently, but a hospital may stipulate that they must work under the supervision of an anesthesiologist. The supervising practitioner accepts medical responsibility for all patient care services provided by a dependent AHP.

Dependent AHPs are not granted clinical privileges (state law and/or hospital bylaws do not allow these individuals to practice independently), so the hospital has flexibility in determining a mechanism for

evaluating them. This evaluation can be done through the human resources department or, depending on their role, these individuals may be formally credentialed and privileged through the medical staff bylaws.

AHPs who provide services in hospitals may come under the hospital's oversight through different routes. The AHP relationship to the hospital may affect how the hospital reviews the professional's qualifications and competence. Some AHPs may be employees of the hospital, and thus are subject to the same hospital policies and procedures as other hospital employees.

AHPs also may be staff who are under contract to provide services but are not employed by the organization. The contract may be between the individual health professional and the hospital, or between the hospital and the agency that employs the health professional. Examples of these include agency staff, nursing pool staff, diagnostic radiology, pathology and clinical laboratory, physical rehabilitation staff (therapists, therapy aides), pharmacists, and clinical dietitians.

Finally, some AHPs who work within the hospital may be employed by a specific practitioner. For example, surgeons may hire surgical nursing staff to assist in operations.

Regardless of the relationship between the hospital and the AHPs, the hospital is ultimately responsible for assessing and ensuring the competence of all AHPs that provide care and services within the hospital. For more on AHPs, see *Joint Commission Guide to Allied Health Professionals.*[14]

Credentialing

Credentialing is defined by the Joint Commission as "the process of obtaining, verifying and assessing the qualifications of a health care practitioner to provide patient care services in or for a health care organization." Credentialing or credentials review, as it sometimes is called, implies that an organization has specified the minimum requirements, or credentials, for entry into medical or other professional staff membership—for example, for granting clinical privileges. Credentials are documented evidence of licensure, education, training, experience, or other qualifications.

Prospective health care practitioners must prove their identity, training, experience, reputation, and competence to the satisfaction of the credentialing committee.

The organization determines through a review of credentials whether an individual meets the requirements. Credentialing also provides information for granting clinical privileges to all LIPs in an organization.

As clear as this may be, the terms *credentialing* and *credentials review* are the source of considerable confusion in health care. This stems from the fact that the terms have different meanings to different individuals and organizations. Sidebar 1-4, The Credentialing Process, on page 11, illustrates the steps involved in the credentialing process.

Privileging

Privileging is the process by which clinical privileges are authorized for a health care practitioner by a health care organization based on evaluation of the individual's credentials and performance. When an individual is granted clinical privileges, he or she is authorized by a health care organization to provide patient care services in or for the organization. Privileging involves the following four distinct activities:

- Determining which clinical procedures or treatments the organization will offer and support;
- Determining what training and experience are required for authorization to perform each clinical procedure or treatment;
- Determining whether applicants for privileges meet these requirements, and officially granting or denying the requested privileges; and
- Monitoring the individuals who are granted privileges to ensure their continued competence and practice within the scope of privileges granted.

The Importance of Credentialing and Privileging

As two of the most crucial assessment activities performed in health care facilities, credentialing and privileging help ensure the provision of quality care. As a result of the proliferation of medical knowledge, the resulting era of specialized medicine, and

---

Sidebar 1-4

The Credentialing Process

Some organizations use the term *credentialing* to describe all of the processes occurring from the time the organization defines the required credentials, to when the health care practitioner applies to the organization, to when he or she is authorized to provide clinical care. The process entails

1. identifying required credentials;
2. notifying the applicant of the required credentials;
3. obtaining applicant's privilege request (and medical staff appointment request, where applicable);
4. collecting credentials;
5. verifying credentials;
6. reviewing credentials;
7. granting privileges; and
8. appointing to medical staff (where applicable).

Most of these steps are covered by the Joint Commission's definition of credentialing, with the exception of points 3, 7, and 8.

---

the litigious nature of modern society, health care organizations must ensure that the practitioners providing care are both qualified and competent to do so. Patient health care outcomes are tied directly to these factors. Credentialing and privileging help assess initial qualifications and evidence of continuing competence.

Problems Associated with Credentialing and Privileging

Inadequate credentialing and privileging can be fraught with future risk management problems for an organization. The process of removing an incompetent practitioner from the organization's list of credentialed and privileged practitioners can be lengthy, emotionally and professionally exhausting, and fiscally damaging to the organization.

Re-credentialing and Re-privileging

Re-credentialing and re-privileging—the reappraisal and renewal of clinical privileges—are steps in the process of continuing privileges. Reappraisal is the review and evaluation of a clinician's adherence to organization requirements and performance of clinical privileges; it leads to a decision regarding reappointment, as applicable, and renewal of privileges. Sometimes referred to as *re-privileging,* the status of a health care practitioner's qualifications is periodically checked. During the credentialing and privileging process, basic information about an applicant's qualifications is reviewed. During the reappraisal and renewal of privileges process, the emphasis is on reviewing information about the practitioner's performance. *Peer review,* the concurrent or retrospective review of a health professional's performance of clinical professional activities by peers through formally adopted written procedures, is integral to this process (see Chapter 5, pages 129-130).

The reappraisal of health care practitioners helps to ensure organizations of the practitioners' competence. Before the 1970s, practitioners were granted hospital privileges on a one-time, life-time basis.[15] Increasing pressure from legal, regulatory, and accrediting bodies quickly made this practice an unwise one for the future. Periodic reevaluations of practitioner qualifications and performance in all types of health care organizations are now mandatory for the protection of patients, practitioners, and organizations alike.

During the initial granting of clinical privileges, the organization uses criteria based on the formal training and education of the applicant, the numbers of procedures performed or patients treated and outcomes, ability to perform the job, and the applicant's current competence. During the renewal of clinical privileges, the criteria focus on current competence. The methods used to verify current competence during the initial granting process are significantly different. For the new applicant, the organization must obtain this information from outside its scope of control. For reappraisal and renewal, however, a majority (and often all) of these data are generally provided from within the organization.

Another major difference in the case of initial granting of privileges is that the applicants must prove their worthiness for privileges. In the reappraisal and renewal process, however, the burden of proof shifts to the organization, which must prove that individuals either continue to be qualified or are no longer qualified to continue their clinical privileges at the current (or increased) level.

Developing a Successful Program for Assessing Competence

High-quality competence assessment programs have a significant impact on organizational performance. They improve patient outcomes, safety, and satisfaction, create an ethos of learning, strengthen relationships between and within departments, enhance the efficient use of resources, increase compliance with regulatory requirements, and improve the hospital's ability to achieve its strategic mission.[16]

The Joint Commission requires accredited hospitals to develop a systematic, objective, and measurable process for competence assessment. Most hospitals satisfy this requirement by developing and implementing a policy, plan, or program to assess, monitor, and improve the competence of all individuals working in or for the hospital. An overview of plan elements is provided below. Details on each component appear in Chapters 2 through 5.

Staffwide Coverage

A successful program for assessing competence covers all individuals working in or for the hospital. This applies to all full-time, part-time, contract, per-diem, evening, night, weekend, relief, and volunteer staff, including LIPs. A person qualified to evaluate the competence of each individual in the skills necessary to perform his or her job should be designated to carry out the assessment. In a successful program, competence assessment is conducted

- at the time of application or hire to determine what orientation and training the individual requires;
- after orientation to determine what assignments or privileges the individual can perform and the need for any further orientation, training, or education;
- whenever the hospital introduces a new service for which employees have been trained, technology, skill requirement, or product; and
- at regular intervals defined by the hospital.

Clear Definition of Competencies, Qualifications, and Expectations

A hospital with a successful competence assessment program defines competencies, qualifications, and performance expectations required for each position. It defines these competencies according to the specific needs of the organization and its patient population, the law, and regulations. When competencies are tied directly to the hospital's strategic mission, vision, and values, individuals who work in the hospital have a better understanding of the organization's objectives, providing the hospital with a powerful tool to drive organizational change and improvement.[16]

Linkage to Training and Professional Development

Because competence assessment is closely linked to training and education, a successful competence assessment program outlines how leaders and department managers continuously explore opportunities for staff learning and professional self-development. The program describes how managers encourage staff members to maintain and continually improve their level of competence and how they encourage personal development and continuing education, both individually and collectively.

Written Job Descriptions

Written job descriptions that define the qualifications for each position, an orientation program outline, performance evaluations, and analysis of competence patterns are also critical elements of a successful competence assessment program. Hospitals must have written job descriptions for all positions. They include the position title and describe all responsibilities and duties associated with it. When developing job descriptions, hospitals should consider any special needs and behaviors of its patient population. For LIPs, a delineation of the clinical privileges outlines the protocols and procedures the practitioner is permitted to perform.

Orientation Programs

An orientation program provides the starting point for the continuing educational development offered by the hospital. The hospital's competence assessment policy should outline the scope of the orientation program, length, time frame, and the actions that will be taken if the individual fails to perform adequately upon conclusion of the program. Proctoring or peer review often is used to ensure that licensed independent practitioners are competent to perform the requested privileges.

Periodic Performance Evaluations

Periodic performance evaluations, based on the requirements identified in the individual job descriptions, are required for all staff members. Evaluations address specific patients' ages and needs and the staff member's success in achieving positive outcomes, as appropriate. A successful competence assessment policy also addresses the means by which competence will be assessed, such as through direct observation, written tests, or record review; the frequency of assessment; the way in which problems identified through assessment will be addressed; and the way by which competence assessment will be documented. For LIPs, reappraisal, re-credentialing, and re-privileging are processes employed to review practitioner performance on a regular basis.

Collection and Analysis of Performance Data

Hospitals are required to regularly collect and analyze data on staff-competence patterns to identify patterns and trends and respond to staff training and education needs. Sources of information include competence assessment results, staff surveys about in-service topics, and performance improvement activities. For example, competence assessment results may indicate that staff are having trouble with a new piece of medical equipment or a new medication administration protocol. As a result, the hospital may decide to develop a new in-service on the equipment or new medication administration protocol. These are referred to as competency maintenance activities.

Grounding in Hospital's Performance Improvement Efforts

Finally, a successful competence assessment program is grounded in the hospital's performance improvement efforts. "Any competency system must define customers' expectations, concentrating on the most important items. Many hospital managers lose sight of the fact that physician credentialing, organization improvement systems, and employee competency assessment all exist to do one thing: increase the likelihood that customer outcome expectations are met," conclude Phillip J. Decker of the University of Houston–Clear Lake and his colleagues.[17] A summary of key steps in establishing a successful competence assessment program is shown in Sidebar 1-5 below, Key Steps in Establishing a Successful Competence Assessment Program.

REFERENCES

1. In Kelly-Thomas KJ: *Clinical and Nursing Staff Development: Current Competence, Future Focus.* Philadelphia: Lippincott Williams and Wilkins, 1998, p 73.
2. Joint Commission: *Comprehensive Accreditation Manual for Hospitals: The Official Handbook.* Oakbrook Terrace, IL: Joint Commission on Accreditation of Healthcare Organizations, 2002.
3. Joint Commission: *Lexicon: Dictionary of Health Care Terms, Organizations, and Acronyms: Second Edition.* Oakbrook Terrace, IL: Joint Commission on Accreditation of Healthcare Organizations, 1998, p 51.
4. Joint Commission: *Credentials Review and Privileging: Questions and Answers for Ambulatory Care.* Oakbrook Terrace, IL: Joint Commission on Accreditation of Healthcare Organizations, 1999, p 23.
5. Joint Commission: *Credentials Review, Clinical Responsibilities, and Competence Assessment: Questions and Answers for Behavioral Health Care Organizations.* Oakbrook Terrace, IL: Joint Commission on Accreditation of Healthcare Organizations, 1999, p 4.
6. McLagan PA: Competencies: The next generation. *Training & Development* May 1997, pp. 40–47.

Sidebar 1-5

Key Steps in Establishing a Successful Competence Assessment Program

Develop a policy outlining all the necessary parts of the program.

- Identify the formal training and/or experience expected of individuals working in the hospital.
- Describe the orientation program.
- Define how competence will be assessed including
  - the methods for determining competence,
  - the frequency, and
  - the methods to be used to correct problems with an individual who fails to perform satisfactorily on the assessment.
- Describe the in-service program, including types of in-service sessions to be provided, and their frequency.
- Describe how external continuing education will be fostered.
- Identify the documentation systems used for each part of the program.

7. Spencer LM, Spencer SM: *Competence at Work.* New York: John Wiley and Sons, 1993. Cited in Decker PJ, Strader MK, Wise RJ: Beyond JCAHO: Using competency models to improve health-care organizations, Part 1. *Hosp Topics* 75(1):23–28, Winter 1997.

8. Decker PJ: The hidden competencies of healthcare: Why self-esteem, accountability, and professionalism may affect customer satisfaction scores. *Hosp Topics* 77(1): 14–26, Winter 1999.

9. Decker PJ, Strader MK, and Wise RJ: Beyond JCAHO: Using competency models to improve healthcare organizations, Part 1. *Hosp Topics* 75(1): 23–28, Winter 1997.

10. Cross T, et al: *Toward a Culturally Competent System of Care, Volume I.* Washington, D.C.: Georgetown University. 1989.

11. Lavizzo-Mourey R., Mackenzie, E. "Cultural Competence: Essential measurements of quality for managed care organizations." *Annals of Internal Medicine*, 124: 919–921. 1996.

12. Wick JY, Zanni GR: Cultural competence: A pragmatic plan for fulfilling a professional imperative. *The Consultant Pharmacist* 16(3): 197–211, Mar 2001.

13. Fortier JP: Multicultural health best practices overview, Nov. 99. Web site: <www.diversityrx.org/HTML/MOCPT1.htm> (accessed March 2002).

14. Joint Commission: *Joint Commission Guide to Allied Health Professionals.* Oakbrook Terrace, IL: Joint Commission on Accreditation of Healthcare Organizations, 2002.

15. Thompson RE: Re-credentialing: Reappointment and renewal of clinical privileges. *Synergy* 25(2): 24–25, 28, Feb 1998.

16. Umiker W: The challenge of competency assessment. *Health Care Supervisor* 17(3): 11–17, Mar 1999.

17. Decker PJ, Strader MK, and Wise RJ: Beyond JCAHO: Using competency models to improve healthcare organizations, Part 2: Developing competence assessment systems. *Hosp Topics* 75(2): 10–17, Spring 1997.

CHAPTER 2

Initial Competence Assessment: Individuals Covered by Human Resources Standards

Competence assessment is a continual process that takes place along a continuum. It begins when leaders define the competencies required of a position and continues with the regular assessment or validation of an individual's competence in the required areas. This chapter addresses the initial stages of competence assessment for individuals covered by the Human Resources standards. It covers how hospitals assess the competence of an individual from application for employment with the organization or a contracted entity through completion of the orientation process.

The initial competence assessment process includes the following five activities:

- The department leader outlines in a job description the performance expectations and competencies required for the specific position.
- The applicant is interviewed and his or her abilities are compared to those outlined in the job description.
- The hospital obtains evidence of the applicant's education, training, licensure, certification, registration, and experience, as applicable.
- The hospital makes a decision to hire or not to hire.
- The hired individual participates and demonstrates competence in hospitalwide and depart-

ment-specific orientation. The hospital provides additional education based on identified learning needs until the individual demonstrates such competence.

A detailed description of each activity follows the outline of JCAHO requirements, below, related to initial competence assessment.

JCAHO Requirements

Hospital leaders are responsible for ensuring both the initial and continuing competence assessment of all staff working in or for the hospital. The Overview section of the Management of Human Resources chapter in the *Comprehensive Accreditation Manual for Hospitals: The Official Handbook (CAMH)* describes the role leaders play in identifying and providing the optimal number of competent staff to meet the needs of patients served by the hospital. The leaders' planning process defines the qualifications, competencies, and staffing necessary to fulfill the hospital's mission. This essential groundwork establishes the criteria against which employees will be assessed. When appropriate, leaders consider special needs and behaviors of specific patient age groups in defining the qualifications, duties, and responsibilities of staff who do not have clinical privileges but who have regular clinical contact with patients. Then, leaders hire competent staff either through traditional employer-employee arrangements or contractual arrangements with other entities (for example, a nursing agency). During an initial assessment, hospital leaders or supervisors review applicants' credentials and qualifications. The applicants' experience, education, and abilities are confirmed during the orientation process. In their role of assessing initial competence of licensed independent practitioners, hospital leaders:

- establish the qualifications and performance expectations for all staff positions;
- ensure that the hospital provides an adequate number of staff members whose qualifications match the job responsibilities;
- ensure that the competence of all staff members is evaluated, maintained, demonstrated, and improved continually;
- establish an orientation process that provides initial job training and information and assesses the staff's ability to fulfill specified responsibilities, and
- sees to it that the hospital assesses each staffer's ability to meet the performance expectations set forth in his or her job description.

A number of these standards describe both the initial and continuing competence assessment process.

Defining Competencies

Leaders establish the competencies that will be required for each individual who works for the hospital. These include general competencies that are necessary for all individuals and those that are specific to the individual's job. A list of competencies should help guide an individual toward the preparation necessary to succeed in a given job. Successful individual performance contributes to the successful performance of the organization as a whole. Competencies will and should vary from hospital to hospital based on factors such as the hospital's mission, vision and

values, patient populations served, patient acuity, and resource capabilities.

In a training article, Timm J. Esque and Thomas F. Gilbert suggest that competencies should meet the following requirements in order to have an impact on organizational performance:

- The information conveyed must accurately describe how individuals can prepare themselves to succeed at their (current or future) jobs;
- Individuals must acquire the competencies needed to succeed at their jobs;
- Individuals must be able to exhibit these acquired competencies in the appropriate sequence at the right times; and
- Individual success on the job must be defined by the requirements for success of the organization. In other words, if the organization is not succeeding, then individuals, by definition, are not succeeding.[1]

Esque's and Gilbert's recommended six-step process for identifying competencies that really matter is shown in Table 2-1 on page 19.

General Competencies

The professional literature is replete with information on generic, general competencies that individuals need for most jobs. Such competencies include professionalism, communication skills, and a focus on the customer. Phillip J. Decker, associate professor of healthcare administration at the University of Houston–Clear Lake, proposes a hierarchy of generic competencies needed specifically in hospitals. Self-esteem, accountability, and professionalism, which he calls "hidden competencies," provide the foundation for others, such as safety, infection control, cost control, patient rights, information management, and others. (See Figure 2-1, Hierarchy of Hospital Generic Competencies, on page 20.) Decker states: "It may be that many of the patient satisfaction and financial struggles that health care executives confront today could be

Table 2-1

A Step-by-Step Process for Identifying Competencies That Really Matter

Step	Questions to Be Answered
1. Define the mission of the job.	What is the ultimate product or service that results from this job?
2. Describe the major outcomes (accomplishments) required to achieve the mission.	What are the necessary and sufficient outcomes that result in achieving the mission of the job?
3. Define performance standards for each major outcome.	• What are the requirements of success for this outcome? • How can each requirement be measured? • How well do the best performers perform against these measures today?
4. Identify known barriers to achieving the performance standards.	• What has prevented people from achieving the standards in the past? • Which barriers, if overcome, will provide the greatest performance improvements?
5. Determine which barriers will be best overcome by training the performer.	Would the barrier best be addressed by: • clarifying performance expectations? • providing performance feedback? • providing better tools? • teaching the individual certain behaviors that will assist in overcoming the known barriers?
6. Develop (or buy) and deliver training.	• What is the briefest training that will allow the individual to overcome the targeted behavior? • Could a job aid be provided instead of training?

SOURCE: Adapted from Esque TJ, Gilbert TF: Making competencies pay off. *Training,* Jan 1995. Used with permission.

solved with some attention to the hidden competencies, without which true customer service, data-based decision making, teamwork, and so on, may not exist."[2] He suggests that if leaders focus on customer outcomes, the following generic competencies will appear in all hospitals for all positions:

- Practices professionalism/customer focus
- Practices information management
- Participates in performance improvement
- Controls costs
- Protects patient rights
- Satisfies patients/customers
- Practices infection control
- Practices safety management.[3]

Other experts outline "core competency categories" in broad areas, such as clinical practice, education, research, management, leadership, ethics and the law, communication and collaboration, diversity, and information technology. The Clinical Center of the Office of Human Resources Management at the National Institutes of Health defines four core competencies in which all Center employees are expected to have a basic level of competence.[4] The behavioral indicators for the competencies safety and emergency preparedness, quality improvement, diversity appreciation and communication, and customer service follow.

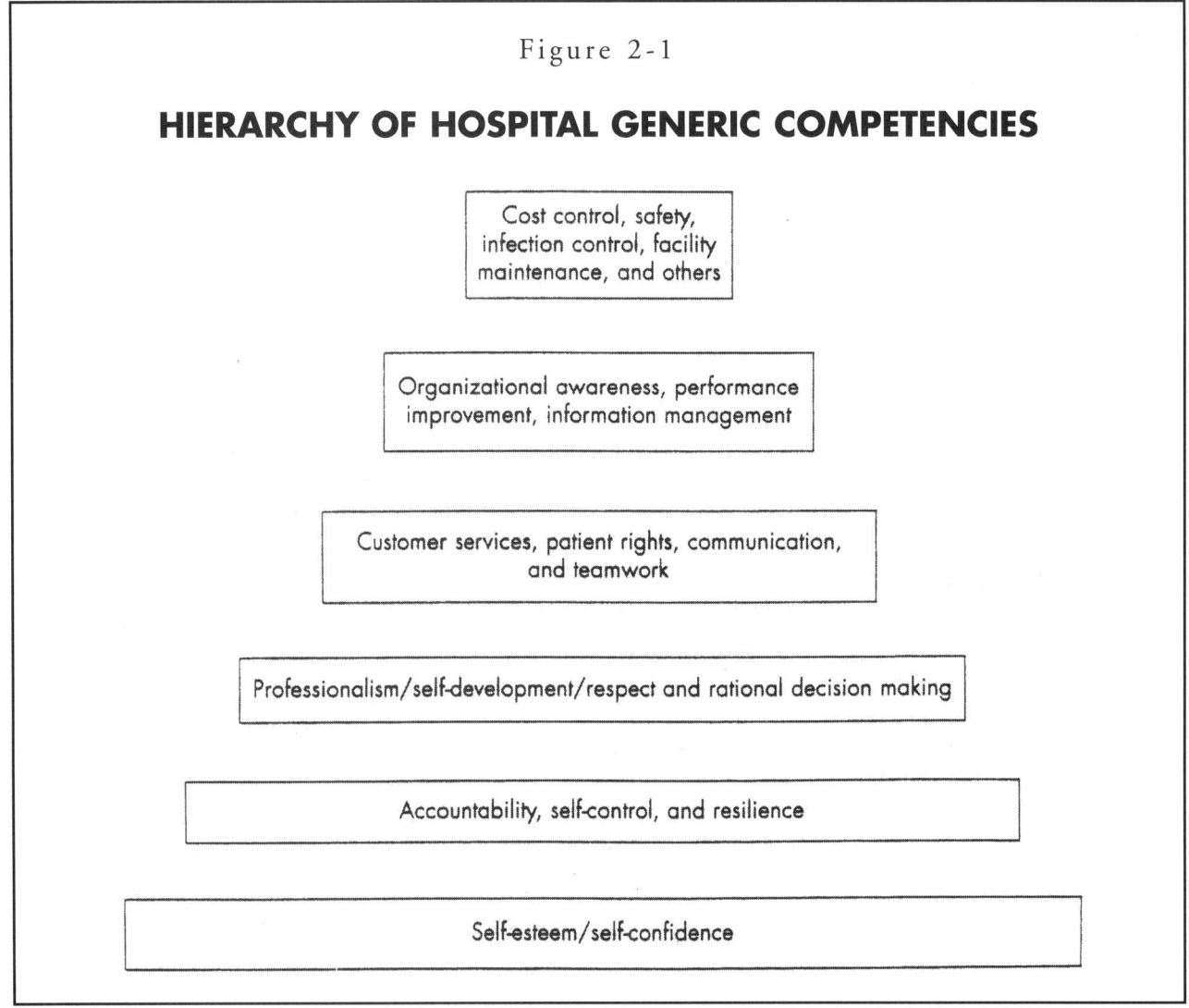

Figure 2-1

HIERARCHY OF HOSPITAL GENERIC COMPETENCIES

Cost control, safety, infection control, facility maintenance, and others

Organizational awareness, performance improvement, information management

Customer services, patient rights, communication, and teamwork

Professionalism/self-development/respect and rational decision making

Accountability, self-control, and resilience

Self-esteem/self-confidence

This hierarchy suggests that professionalism, accountability, and self-esteem serve as the foundation for other health care competencies.
SOURCE: Decker PJ: The hidden competencies of healthcare: Why self-esteem, accountability, and professionalism may affect hospital customer satisfaction scores. *Hosp Topics* 77(1): 14–26, Winter 1999. Used with permission.

Safety and Emergency Preparedness

- engages in proper safety, emergency preparedness, and infection control practices;
- demonstrates and/or describes how to respond to an emergency involving a life-threatening medical condition, security incident, failure of a critical building utility, fire or other hazardous materials incident; and
- demonstrates or describes appropriate measures for preventing the spread of infection.

Quality (or Performance) Improvement

- provides quality service in all endeavors by supporting initiatives designed to improve individual and organizational performance;
- understands, verbalizes and participates in the quality improvement process, especially as it relates to customer service; and
- demonstrates knowledge of the Clinical Center's strategic mission, vision, and guiding principals.

Diversity Appreciation and Communication

- effectively communicates and interacts with patients, their families, and other external and internal customers (including fellow employees) from diverse backgrounds;
- anticipates, assesses, and responds effectively to the needs of diverse customers both internal and external, making excellent customer service the first priority;
- listens to others, asks for clarification when needed, and expresses one's own point in an objective and issue-oriented manner;
- is alert for and constructively challenges inappropriate or offensive behaviors;
- encourages diverse opinions and ideas when engaged in work projects or hospital activities;
- provides access to translator or translation services when necessary; and
- uses appropriate hospital services designated when needed to communicate with employees and patients who have speech and hearing disorders.

Customer Service

- anticipates, assesses, and responds effectively to the needs of diverse customers both internal and external, making excellent customer service the first priority;
- promotes courtesy to customers through the use of verbal amenities;
- promptly answers telephone with identification of self and service;
- demonstrates active listening by acknowledging and clarifying verbal messages to ensure mutual understanding;
- seeks information to better understand customer needs and requests;
- proactively keeps customers informed by giving timely and appropriate feedback;
- assesses problem situations and initiates effective service interventions that result in customer satisfaction (that is, informs patients about delays);
- diffuses sensitive or difficult customer situations and creates a climate for mutual problem solving;
- explores ways of accommodating different customer requests, cultural practices, and age progression in order to provide sensitive customer service;
- demonstrates through daily interactions that all individuals in the Center are customers; and
- coordinates role with staff in other departments in order to effectively meet customer service needs.

Each hospital should develop its own competencies checklist or outline that reflects its mission, vision, value, patient population, policies and procedures, and all applicable laws and regulations. The above list is one of many possibilities.

Departmental or Job-Specific Competencies

The competencies required for each position should be defined according to the specific job responsibilities, law and regulation, and the specific needs of the hospital. All positions—including those filled by temporary staff, volunteers, regular employees, and contract staff—should have defined competencies.

For example, to identify those competencies required of pharmacists who provide services under contract and those who are directly employed, one medical center convened a work group of pharmacists and administrators.[5] The group identified clinical information retrieval as one skill in which all pharmacists should be able to demonstrate competence. The group stated the general competence rule for clinical information retrieval as, "The pharmacist uses available on-line systems for clinical information retrieval." This rule reflected the needs of the hospital and specific job responsibilities.

Job descriptions and practice guidelines help establish specific competencies. A job description identifies the qualifications required for the position. It describes both the routine and special expectations of the job. This document can be used as a starting point in determining the competencies required for the position and serves as a tool in the process of assessing an individual's competence in the position.

Elements of a Job Description. Written job descriptions that define the qualifications and performance expectations in measurable terms for each position are necessary and required. They should include the position title, supervisory relationships (title of supervisor and titles of those supervised) and a description of all responsibilities and essential and nonessential duties. These duties include those that directly affect the individual's performance of his or her responsibilities—such as direct care—and those that do not, such as participation in in-services.

A job description should also include qualifications, including education, license(s), experience, knowledge/skills, and physical/emotional expectations. The hospital must maintain a written job description for all personnel hired through contractual

arrangements. Examples 2-1 and 2-2 on pages 37 through 50 are sample job or position descriptions from two different organizations: a sample chief privacy officer job description from the American Health Information Management Association (AHIMA), and an OR Staff Nurse job description from Rockingham Memorial Hospital. Each outlines the educational requirements and qualifications needed for the job as well as specific responsibilities. Example 2-2 is a job description, a performance appraisal tool, and a competency evaluation form all in one.

Although not required, hospitals may find it beneficial to include performance rules in position descriptions. Linking performance rules to key responsibilities can help to clarify position expectations. Useful performance rules are

- defined in terms that are observable and measurable;
- linked directly to the key function specified in the position or job description;
- consistent with the hospital's mission and values and the needs of those served by the position; and
- regularly reviewed for current performance.

Practice Guidelines and Standards of Care. Practice guidelines and standards of care are rapidly evolving as objective criteria for measuring competence and in assisting leaders in defining the competencies required of a particular job. They involve an observable process and result in a measurable outcome. Practice guidelines, sometimes called clinical protocols or clinical pathways, link patient conditions or diagnoses to processes, procedures, and outcomes and reduce variation in the provision of care. A rule of care is any treatment rule formally established by the hospital. When adopted by the clinical leaders, practice guidelines become the rule of care for the "typical" patient within a diagnostic or symptom-defined group. A clinician who provides patient care is expected to conform to the rules established by the guidelines.

Competencies for Special Patient Populations

In defining job-specific qualifications, duties, responsibilities, and competencies, leaders should consider the unique growth and development needs of the hospital's patient population. There must be evidence that the special needs and behaviors of specific patient age groups were considered when determining the qualifications that an individual must bring to the position or the abilities that the individual needs to possess to be considered an acceptable candidate for an assignment.

Leaders initiate the process of defining competencies for special patient populations through the following four activities:
• Defining services provided by the organization;
• Defining the patient population served;
• Identifying age and special needs groups within each population; and
• Identifying the staff delivering these services.

A description of each activity follows.

Defining Services. The hospital's mission and vision statement provide a starting place for the definition of services to be provided. Major service categories, such as emergency care, maternity services, and neurology services, can be defined and the specific services outlined within each category. For example, within the emergency care category, specific services might include radiology services, pharmacy services, and nutritional services.

Defining Patient Population. The mission statement, patient demographics, departmental organization, case mix data, diagnostic related groups (DRGs), and utilization patterns provide information related to the patient population served by the hospital. Many hospitals choose to delineate four patient categories: neonatal and infant, child and adolescent, adult, and geriatric. If the hospital has specialty age units (for example, newborn nursery,

pediatric, geriatric), these may provide a logical starting place.

Specialty hospitals, such as pediatric hospitals, may choose to identify patient groups by growth and developmental stages unique to pediatrics (for example, premature, newborn, infants from birth to one year of age, toddler, pre-school, and so forth).

Care-specific criteria (for example, ventilator-dependent) offer a different approach to defining patient populations. In fact, because the organization of pediatric care has shifted to service units rather than age-specific units, patient groups might be defined as "patients requiring oncology services," "patients requiring cardiology services," and so forth. Sidebar 2-1, Common Patient–Population Groupings Used to Define Special Patient Population Competencies, page 24, summarizes common groupings. Each hospital should choose groupings that make sense for the organization. The Joint Commission expects organizations to define the population they serve in this manner.

Identifying Age and Special Needs Groups. The most direct way of identifying the special needs and behaviors of specific patient age groups is to identify the physical, motor and sensory, cognitive, and psychosocial characteristics of each patient population. Needs associated with these characteristics can then be defined and interventions designed to meet the needs.

For example, one characteristic of the psychosocial development of adolescents is their desire for privacy. Thus, in a radiology department, staff must be aware of privacy concerns and provide appropriately for them. Another example is the characteristic in the psychosocial development of infants at the age of seven or eight months of fearing strangers. Thus, infants must have their parents or primary caregivers at hand at all possible times. Appropriate interventions include involving

Common Patient-Population Groupings Used to Define Special Patient Population Competencies

Common groupings used to define patient populations are by chronological age, functional age, or life stages.

- *Chronological age groupings* group people by years. For example, a general acute care hospital might define its age groupings as infants, toddlers, pre-school children, school-age children in grades K through 6, adolescents, and adults age 19 and up.
- *Functional age groupings* are based on patients' physical appearances and ability to perform expected tasks such as activities of daily living. Categories might include dependence or independence in activities of daily living.
- *Life stage groupings* are perhaps the most common type of age-specific groupings. These are broad categories based on the expected or ideal physical, psychological, and social attributes of a group of people in a range of chronological years.

parents in procedures, keeping parents within the infant's sight, and limiting the number of strangers caring for the infant.

Competencies for special patient populations should be based directly on the specific patient needs and characteristics identified by the hospital. With the lists of patient needs and staff categories as a resource, the hospital should list the broad education, training,

skill, and aptitude needed to carry out the responsibilities of the position. It should also define special requirements and specific tasks that staff members must carry out to meet patient needs. Department managers most often are best suited to devise the list of skills and qualifications required for individuals rendering care to patients in this population.

Identifying Staff. Each hospital can delineate the staff delivering specific patient care services in a similar fashion. Because competence assessment requirements apply to all care and service staff, the hospital's leaders should define as comprehensively as possible all professional or other staff who deliver care to the patient or those whose work affects patient care. Brainstorming can be used effectively as a method to identify the staff involved in delivery of each care or service. Hospitals must remember to include volunteers, per diem staff, evening staff, weekend staff, and contract staff, and any other staff whose work affects delivery of care.

Consulting Practice Guidelines. Hospitals may also wish to consult practice guidelines developed by professional organizations, protocols, textbooks, and critical pathways for age and disability-specific competence requirements. For example, the American Dietetic Association offers age-specific practice guidelines covering nutritional care of patients from birth through adulthood. Nursing texts provide guidance on administering intramuscular injections to children and the elderly, covering such topics as needle sizes, site selection, and technique. Drug companies provide age-specific medical use evaluation guidelines for medications. Health care associations can also be a source of published age-specific requirements.

For quick and repeated reference, many hospitals find it helpful to develop charts that visually link the needs of special patient populations with staff competence expectations. Examples of such charts are the adult and geriatric characteristics and competency expectations developed by Upper

Chesapeake Health System-Harford Memorial Hospital, Maryland, Example 2-3 on pages 51 and 52, and Example 2-4 on pages 53–55, which illustrates the similar competencies defined by River Parishes hospital for radiology department staff.

Cultural Competencies

In defining job-specific qualifications, duties, responsibilities, and competencies, leaders also should consider the unique cultural backgrounds of the hospital's patient population. Patients have a fundamental right to care that safeguards their personal dignity and respects their cultural, psychological, and spiritual values. Those caring for patients must be sensitive and responsive to these areas of a patient's needs.

Influences of Individual Cultural Differences. This requirement is reflected in numerous Joint Commission standards. For example, Assessment of Patients standards describe the importance of a patient's cultural context, family context, and background in determining his or her response to illness and treatment. The Education of Patients standards and intents specify that patient education activities provided by hospitals should be appropriate to the cultural characteristics of the patients concerned. The Care of Patients requirements describe how care must be appropriate to the patient's needs, as defined during the assessment process.

Individual cultural differences can influence healthcare-related issues such as birth rituals and beliefs, family participation in care delivery, dietary beliefs and practices, alternative health care practices, and religiously founded beliefs and practices about death and dying.

Moreover, areas of potential cultural differences with respect to language and communication, such as the interpretation of and response to silence, to touch or physical contact, or to eye contact, can have major ramifications for clinicians who care for patients from cultures different than their own.

According to Casie Williams, RN, an expert in Native American culture, "Non-verbal communication is culturally-specific and affected by beliefs, values, social rules, and communication premises. Miscommunication can occur when definitions of another culture are used for interpreting meaning."

Williams cites a number of examples. For example, to an Inuit (Alaskan Native American), head nodding means "I hear what you are saying." To a non-Inuit, the meaning may be "I understand what you are saying." To an Inuit, a furrowed brow means "No" or "I'm displeased with you." To a non-Inuit, the meaning may be "I'm listening very carefully to what you are saying" or "I question the truth in what I am seeing or hearing."[6] Inuit communication patterns differ widely from non-Inuit patterns. For instance, before an Inuit answers a question, there may be long pauses as he or she thinks about the response. In contrast, non-Inuits tend to communicate responses rapidly. Staff who provide care to different people of different cultures must be educated about relevant cultural beliefs, values, and social rules.

Cultural Differences in Reporting Pain. Another example of wide cultural variation is the reporting of pain, an issue critical to effective pain assessment and management. Dennis C. Turk, PhD, the John and Emma Bonica professor of Anesthesiology and Pain Research at the University of Washington in Seattle, cautions caregivers to beware of the "patient uniformity myth"—the tendency to treat patients who have the same diagnosis and are in pain as a homogenous group, despite the huge variations in culture, age, ethnicity, and other factors.[7] Certain individuals believe that reporting pain is a sign of weakness, for example. Says Albert Ray, MD, president of the American Academy of Pain Medicine and medical director of the Miami Pain and Integrative Medicine Center, "As practitioners, we need to be aware of what our own culture, values, and mores are telling us about a person in pain. The more we can concentrate on the patient and clear out our own judgmental perspectives, the better off we[and the patient] will be."[8]

Population-based Health Statistics. Population-based health statistics is another factor that relates to cultural competence in the delivery of health care. Writing on the importance of cultural competence to the pharmacist's practice, Jeannette Y. Wick, RPh and Guido R. Zanni, PhD, cite the variation of disease states by racial and ethnic groups, such as the disproportionate prevalence among African Americans of cardiovascular disease, diabetes, and other disease states, and the high incidence of cervical cancer in Vietnamese women in the United States.[9] They also cite the effect that different attitudes can have on treatment outcomes, such as the belief among some Hispanic groups that breast cancer is related to breast trauma or use of drugs and alcohol, beliefs that may add an element of shame or impede timely screening.[10]

Defining Cultural Competencies. How does a hospital define the cultural competencies required of individuals working for the organization? The hospital leadership can begin by defining the services provided by the organization, the patient population served, special cultural beliefs, values, and communication systems within each population, and the staff that delivers services to each population. It can also ensure that the ethnicity of the patients served is properly recorded. Many patients will have multiple racial and ethnic identities, each of which should be identified.[11] Cultural competence permeates seven domains of a health care organization's activities as outlined in Table 2-2, Seven Domains of Cultural Competence, page 27.

Competency requirements of clinicians in assessing pain, for example, should include understanding the meaning of the pain to the patient, believing the patient, and maintaining a non-judgmental attitude. These culturally specific competence requirements complement job-specific and special

needs and behavior-specific competence requirements. Examples include understanding pain transmission and pain perception, knowing what pain treatments are available based on the patient's unique needs and behaviors, and offering a variety of pharmacological—invasive and non-invasive— and non-pharmacological options.

Documenting Competencies

After leaders define the cultural competencies required of each position, the competencies must be documented. Methods include listing the competencies in the position or job description, an addendum to the position or job description, a unit or service policy, a defined peer review process, a contract between the hospital and the contracted agency or provider group, and performance reviews.

Assessing Abilities and the Interview Process

After the performance expectations and competencies required for a specific position have been determined, candidates apply for the job, are interviewed, and their qualifications are compared to the job requirements outlined in the job description. The application form itself contains information about the applicant's education, training, licensure, certification, registration, and experience, as applicable. This information must be verified. A supplemental employment application for the recreational therapy department of UNC Health Care is illustrated in Example 2-5. (See pages 56-59 at the end of this chapter.) It requests a list of interventional skills in which competence has been demonstrated. After the application form has been reviewed, a promising candidate is contacted for an interview.

Comparing Skills Against a Job Description

A thorough comparison between the job description and a candidate's skills and competencies is

Table 2-2

Seven Domains of Cultural Competence

1. *Values and attitudes.* The hospital's leaders should promote mutual respect, awareness of the varying degrees of acculturation, a patient-centered perspective, and acceptance that beliefs may influence a patient's response to health, illness, disease, and death.

2. *Communication styles.* The hospital's leaders should promote sensitivity, awareness, knowledge, and alternatives to written communication.

3. *Community/patient participation.* The hospital's leaders should promote continuous, active involvement of patients and community leaders and members.

4. *Physical environment, materials, and resources.* The hospital's leaders should ensure culturally and linguistically friendly interior design, pictures, posters, and artwork as well as magazines, brochures, audio, video, and films. Print information should be literacy sensitive and congruent with the culture and the language of patient populations served.

5. *Policies and procedures.* Written policies, procedures, mission statements, goals, and objectives should incorporate linguistic and cultural principles, as should clinical protocols, orientation, community involvement, and outreach. The staff should be as multicultural and multilingual as possible, reflecting the community.

6. *Population-based clinical practice.* Culturally skilled clinicians avoid stereotyping while appreciating the importance of culture. They know their own worldviews, learn about populations, understand sociopolitical influences, and practice appropriate intervention skills and strategies.

7. *Training and professional development.* The hospital's leaders should promote training and professional development in the area of cultural competence.

SOURCE: Adapted from *Cultural Competence: A Journey.* Bureau of Primary Health Care. Health Resources and Services Administration, U.S. Dept. of Health and Human Services, nd.

critical. Hospital staff must obtain evidence of the applicant's education, training, licensure, certification, registration, and experience, as applicable. Human resources staff should thoroughly corroborate the backgrounds and professional preparation of every applicant, particularly those who potentially will be involved in direct care. Meticulous background checking is critical. Although treatment staff have the closest interaction with patients, support staff also perform tasks that bring them into direct contact with patients. Hospitals should carefully review the backgrounds of support staff and ensure their competence in performing job responsibilities.

Specificity of Information. Documentation of competence from a previous employer must be specific to the area of competence required in the hospital. For high-risk procedures or treatments, it is useful to request information on the applicant's current competence specific to that responsibility. A generic reference, such as "the staff member is a competent nurse," is not sufficiently specific; nor is a skills checklist or a self-assessment.

The hospital must verify any self-assessment. Reviews of records and observation logs could establish whether the staff member is proficient in documenting procedures, such as notification of physicians and communication with other professionals. See Table 2-3 below, Appropriate Evidence of Competence.

After hospital staff have interviewed the applicant and obtained the appropriate evidence of his or her qualifications for the position, staff make a decision to hire or not. They extend an offer to the top candidate and arrange for a start date.

The Orientation Process

Orientation is a major component of competence assessment. The Joint Commission requires hospitals to have an orientation process that provides each individual who works for the hospital with initial job training and information and assesses the individual's ability to fulfill specified responsibilities. The process familiarizes new staff members with their jobs and the work environment before they begin patient care or other activities. Orientation emphasizes specific job-related aspects of patient safety, thereby helping to ensure safe and effective job performance.

Who Should Receive Orientation

All staff members should receive orientation, including volunteers, business office staff, students, contract workers, all types of allied health professionals,

Table 2-3

Appropriate Evidence of Competence

Appropriate evidence of competence will vary for the new staff member and those experienced with the hospital. Evidence of competence could include but is not limited to the following:

- Type of education (high school diploma, bachelor's degree, master's degree);
- Special certification (peripherally-inserted central catheter line, oncology certified nurse);
- Length of experience (two years med/surg, ER, oncology/chemotherapy, pediatrics);
- Knowledge testing (eg, pharmacology test, nutrition test, general knowledge test);
- Self-assessment (this is an individual's impression of his or her competence and may not be completely accurate);
- Interviews in which staff describe types of patients, diagnoses, and procedures in their previous work experience;
- In-services or continuing education attended;
- Letters of reference from qualified individuals specifically addressing competence;
- Previous competence assessments or performance evaluations;
- Direct observation;
- Preceptored or supervisory visits;
- Formal peer review, including observations and record review; and
- Narrative/anecdotal comments in personnel files and performance reviews.

and agency personnel. Each individual who works for the hospital should learn what to do in an emergency—such as a fire—and how to protect patient confidentiality and patient rights, among other topics. This does not include personnel whose services are not directly related to patient care, such as repair personnel, delivery personnel, and personnel who service equipment and provide services periodically. However, forensic staff must be oriented and educated about their responsibilities related to patient care.

A hospital should have well-defined policies and procedures outlining the type of orientation required for individuals working for the organization. Orientation is a two- or three-stage process that covers general hospitalwide job competencies and specific departmental and position competencies. Topics covered in each stage should be outlined in the hospital's overall competence assessment plan or policies. Department- and job-specific orientations should not duplicate what is covered in the general orientation, but should complement and supplement it with more specific material related the individual's specific role.

Orientation Topics

Topics for each stage of the orientation process reflect the hospitalwide, department-specific, and job-specific competencies defined by leaders before hiring the individual or bringing him or her into the organization. General hospitalwide orientation provides information that is critical to all individuals, wherever they work for the organization. It usually includes topics such as

- hospital mission, vision, and values;
- performance improvement program;
- safety and emergency management policies and procedures;
- work environment and environment of care;
- infection control policies and procedures; and
- benefits and personnel policies.

Emergency Management Orientation. In view of the September 11, 2001, terrorist attacks and anthrax poisonings that occurred in the weeks following the attacks, emergency management has assumed increased importance for all types of health care organizations. Table 2-4, below, Essential Topics for Emergency Management Orientation, outlines topics for emergency management orientation as required by the Joint Commission.

Table 2-4

Essential Topics for Emergency Management Orientation

Orientation for all personnel who participate in implementing the hospital's emergency management plan should address the following, as appropriate to the individual:
- Specific roles and responsibilities during emergencies;
- How to recognize specific types of emergencies (for example, an emergency management nurse should receive training on the symptoms caused by agents that may be used in chemical or bioterrorist attacks);
- The information and skills required to perform assigned duties during emergencies;
- The backup communication system used during emergencies; and
- How supplies and equipment are obtained during emergencies.

Department-Specific Orientation. Department-specific orientation generally includes such topics as
- departmental policies and procedures;
- patient-safety issues, policies, and procedures;
- description of the key functions and tasks performed in the department or unit;
- equipment and skills needed for the tasks;
- job-specific safety issues; and
- the individual's role in the department.

Job-Specific Orientation. Job-specific orientation generally includes such topics as
- elements of the individual's job description;
- specific performance expectations and competencies; and
- skills and equipment use specific to the position that will be validated by a manager or supervisor.

Competence Assessment During Orientation

A hospital's orientation process includes an evaluation of the individual's ability to perform the job for which he or she has been hired. Assessment of the individual's competence to perform specific assigned duties during the orientation process establishes a baseline. Some hospitals use a skills self-assessment inventory. Example 2-6, "Alaska Native Medical Center Nursing Service Skills Self-assessment Inventory" on pages 60–63 is one such document. This inventory, along with the supervisor's or proctor's assessment, helps to define the education or training that is needed in order for the individual to attain competence. At the end of the orientation process, the individual must be competent to perform the skills specified in his or her job description.

The importance of developing and implementing a competency-based orientation process is described frequently in the professional literature.[11-13] During the orientation process at one hospital's heart center, for example, both managers and current staff instruct and develop each new perioperative cardiovascular nurse in the various skills required to

perform the job safely and effectively.[11] The new team members must demonstrate mastery of these skills before their orientation is completed. They are offered specific learning options, such as reading material, observation of demonstrations, different types of quizzes, and tours, for each performance criterion, and then are evaluated on specific practice criterion, such as assisting in draping the cardiac patient. Evaluation methods include interviews, quizzes, demonstrations, and so forth. Example 2-7, Selected Practice Criteria for Cardiovascular Operating Room Nurses, page 64, shows selected performance criteria, learning options, and evaluation methods for cardiovascular operating room nurses.

According to the center's assistant director, Mariece Huffman, RN, CNOR, because new nurses come from different backgrounds, there is an emphasis on individualized orientation. New employees are urged to take responsibility for identifying and communicating their learning needs and to take the initiative in seeking learning opportunities.[11]

The orientation process described in the literature for nurses in another hospital includes a one-day hospitalwide orientation, followed by a three-and-a-half-day competency-based orientation coordinated by the centralized nursing education department.[14] Beth Israel Deaconess Medical Center's nurse manager of transplant, hemodialysis and organ acquisition, Christine R. Boylan, MSN, RN, and Rosemary Westra, MS, RN, coordinator of performance improvement, state that "[The] orientation assesses the nurses' current ability to meet identified standards for competent performance and serves as a basis for developing an orientation plan to bridge the gap between current ability and their stated role expectations."[14] Nurses must meet performance expectations in three key areas: critical thinking/decision making, technical skills, and interpersonal/communication skills. Assessment methods include role-playing, video- and audiotapes, simulated skills labs, and other methods.

Instructional Methods for Orientation. Instructional or educational methods used during orientation should be varied based on the content to be taught and can include lectures or classes, videos, written materials, group discussions, one-on-one instruction, demonstration, return demonstration, gaming, simulation, role-playing, role-modeling, self-instruction, and computer-assisted self-directed instruction.[15] Learning experts indicate that the use of multiple learning methods increases the likelihood that skills will be acquired and retained. Learners tend to retain more if they discuss and perform a skill than if they simply read about it, hear about it, or see it demonstrated. Experts have developed numerous methods for teaching competencies based on theories of adult education, social learning, and other theoretical learning models.[16]

Training and education are provided during orientation to help individuals obtain the skills, knowledge, and abilities needed to meet a competency requirement. Assessment verifies that the competency is met after the orientation and continues to be met. Competence must be assessed by a person qualified to perform the assessment. Appropriate assessment tools or methods vary according to the skill being assessed. Written tests or quizzes, documentation review, role-playing, verbalization, observation and demonstration, interactive multimedia, and other methods can be used to assess specific competencies.

Who Performs the Assessment? Before an individual demonstrates a competency independently, a qualified person must assess the individual and deem him or her competent to perform that skill independently. This applies even when the individual has performed the skill independently in previous jobs. If the skill is performed infrequently in the job, and the individual's competence in this skill is not assessed on completion of the orientation session, competence must be proven before the individual performs the skill independently.

Who is qualified to perform the assessment and who should determine acceptable and unacceptable responses to competence questions? A supervisor will most likely be responsible for the assessment and for determining acceptable and unacceptable responses to age-specific and other competence questions during or following the orientation session. However, someone other than the supervisor should be responsible if the supervisor does not have clinical or technical expertise in the competency being assessed. Hospital leaders should identify such exceptions and determine how the need for assessment and observation will be addressed.

If no one in the organization has the training or experience to appropriately assess a specific skill set, what should leaders do? This situation most often arises when a service—for example, speech therapy—is provided by a single individual under contract. In such an instance, it may help to examine the skills to be assessed. Identify those that are unique to the individual's training and experience and those that could realistically be assessed by another staff person. Only those skills unique to the profession may need to be assessed by a professional working in the same discipline.

When skills must be assessed by someone who works in the same discipline, the individual's professional association should be contacted. The association may have developed tests or might identify other similarly trained professionals who could come on site to perform a peer review after orientation. Community colleges and other health care organizations may also be resources.

All individuals must be assessed after completing the orientation process. Documentation of the validation of an individual's competencies during and following orientation is critical. The supervisor's or proctor's observations must be documented after an employee's orientation.

Contract and Volunteer Personnel

The standards in the Human Resource chapter apply to direct, contract, and volunteer personnel who provide patient care services on behalf of a hospital. Patient care personnel can include, but are not limited to, nursing, therapy, dietary, pharmacy, activities staff, drug and alcohol counselors, and nursing assistants/aides. Patient services personnel can include, but are not limited to, homemakers, companions, sitters, chore workers, drivers, and home medical equipment delivery and repair technicians. Non-patient care or service personnel who would not be included are, for example, volunteers who

- deliver the mail or flowers;
- staff the information desk, gift shop or offer library services;
- perform patient errands such as writing and mailing letters or obtaining magazines and toiletries from the gift shop;
- conduct marketing or fund-raising activities; or
- provide simple wheelchair transport services such as discharging patients.

Managing Contracted Services

Hospitals must manage contracted services and personnel just as they manage those provided by direct employees. This also applies to volunteers. They can either spell out criteria for performance of the service in the contract or policy, or they can review and adopt the contract organization's policies and practices.

The organization should have verified information (where relevant) of the following for all contract and volunteer personnel:

- Education and training consistent with applicable legal and regulatory requirements and organizational policy;
- Evidence of license, certification, or registration, when applicable;
- Evidence that an individual's knowledge, experience, and competence are appropriate for his or her assigned responsibilities as required by

the contracting organization;
- Orientation to the hospital;
- Evaluations of performance;
- Health status as required by job responsibilities, as defined by the hospital, and as required by laws and regulations;
- Criminal background check or pre-employment verification of no convictions for abuse or neglect, when required by laws and regulations and if indicated by the patient population (for example, pediatric and psychiatric); and
- References, when applicable.

Evidence of verification is illustrated in Sidebar 2-2, Evidence of Verification for Contracted Personnel, page 33.

Hiring Contract Staff

When hiring contract staff, the hospital should
- define the required qualifications for the contract staff. This should be delineated in the contract language.
- review the personnel practices of the organization under contract and its staff's qualifications to determine whether staff comply with the hospital's requirements. If the organization's practices, such as hiring, orientation, and development of job descriptions, are acceptable, the hospital can extend approval to the contracted personnel for the services to be provided. If the practices are not acceptable, the hospital can define in the contract the specific requirements, or perform the requirements.
- develop mechanisms to ensure that the organization under contract complies with the hospital's requirements.

Hospitals are responsible for retaining information for active and former contracted personnel and determining where it is stored.

What Surveyors Look For

The Joint Commission evaluates a hospital's competence assessment process by reviewing policies, procedures, and plans that are verified through interviews, observation, and the examination of documents and records. Initial and continuing assessment of competence is covered in many activities throughout the survey, including leadership interviews, the human resources interview, review of personnel records, and on-site visits. This section covers the items that surveyors look for in assessing a hospital's initial competence assessment process.

The Leadership Interview

During the leadership interview, the surveyor asks leaders to describe the hospital's process for defining, assessing, maintaining, demonstrating, and improving the competence of all staff members on a continuing basis. This discussion focuses on the planning and overall operation of the process. For all leaders, questions specific to initial competence assessment might include the following:

- How do you define the qualifications, responsibilities, competencies, and staffing needed to carry out the hospital's mission?
- How do you ensure that organizations under contract that provide personnel are complying with all Joint Commission Human Resources standards requirements?

For departmental or service directors, questions specific to assessing initial competence might include the following:

- How do you define the qualifications and responsibilities of staff?
- What system have you implemented to evaluate how well those responsibilities are met and the number of staff needed to fulfill the mission for their respective areas?
- How are staff oriented to their department, job responsibilities, and performance expectations?
- How do directors determine whether staff are competent to perform assigned duties and, when appropriate, provide care for the special needs and behaviors of specific age groups?

Sidebar 2-2

Evidence of Verification for Contracted Personnel

Evidence of verification for contracted personnel includes

- appropriate information for each contracted person maintained by the contracting organization/individual;
- copies of appropriate information for each contracted person obtained from the contracted organization/individual;
- the results of an audit of appropriate information for contracted individuals conducted by the contractor—the hospital determines whether to include a percentage or all contracted individuals in the audit; and
- the results of an audit of personnel, health, and education records of contracted individuals conducted by the contracted organization. In this case, the hospital defines the specific information to be included in the audit and whether the audit is to include a percentage or all contracted individuals. Note: The audit must include an attestation as to the accuracy of the information. A simple attestation letter indicating that the information is current and on file at the organization site, without the audit is not sufficient.

For nursing leaders, questions specific to assessing initial competence might include the following:

- How have the nursing leaders defined the nursing staff's qualifications and responsibilities?
- What system have they implemented to evaluate how well those responsibilities are fulfilled?

- How do nursing leaders ensure that the hospital employs nursing staff whose qualifications are commensurate with defined job responsibilities and applicable licensure, laws and regulations, or certification?
- How are staff oriented to their department, job responsibilities, and performance expectations?

The Human Resources Interview

During the human resources interview, the surveyor also asks about the initial and continuing competence assessment process. The emphasis here is how the planned process is implemented on a day-to-day basis. The surveyor addresses such issues as the orientation provided to new staff and the actions that are taken when a staff member is found to be not competent. Questions specific to initial competence assessment might include the following:

- How are job descriptions developed?
- How do you verify educational and training requirements and, as applicable, evidence of current licensure, certification, or registration?
- How do leaders determine whether work assignments are consistent with individuals' qualifications?
- How are staff oriented to the hospital, their department, their specific job responsibilities, and the performance expectations of that job?
- How do you orient, train, assign responsibilities to, and evaluate volunteers accepted by the hospital?
- For forensic services, what education and training do you provide to staff who have no clinical training or experience but who interact with patients?

Review of Personnel Records

During the review of personnel records, the surveyor looks at a sample of records or other documents taken from all levels and all areas, when applicable, for evidence of licensure and certification (where applicable); references; documented experience; and completed competence review forms. The surveyor pays particular attention to the process for ensuring follow-up on licensure expirations. Sidebar 2-3, The Survey of Information Related to Contracted Personnel and Volunteer Staff, page 35, summarizes the steps that surveyors may take to ascertain a hospital's use of contracted personnel or volunteers for patient care and/or services.

Interviewing Clinical and Support Staff

During visits to services or units, the surveyor may interview a cross section of clinical and support/administrative staff that provide care or services regarding how staff are oriented and trained to ensure initial competence. Questions asked of staff might include:

- How do your leaders define the qualifications and responsibilities of staff who work in this setting?
- Do staff members receive an orientation to the department and initial job training and information? Please describe.
- How does the department manager determine whether staff are competent to perform assigned duties and, when appropriate, provide care for the special needs and behaviors of specific age groups?

Common Problems in Assessing Competence

Various aspects of competence assessment have posed problems for many accredited hospitals. Results from recent surveys indicate that two facets of competence assessment raise red flags in almost every health care setting. The first involves who is covered by the competence assessment process; the second involves who is qualified to assess competence.

Many hospitals include only full-time and/or direct-care staff members in their competence assessment process, neglecting to assess the competence of contract, part-time, volunteer, and on-call staff. It is important to remember that the Joint Commission Human Resources standards require assessment and maintenance of competence for all individuals who provide care or services.

Improvement Tips

The following tips, if followed by a hospital, can minimize the chances that an organization will fail to meet the JCAHO standards of compliance in the area of initial competence assessment:

- Review the hospital's plan for competence assessment to ensure that it includes all clinical and non-clinical staff, including full- and part-time employees, contracted staff, and volunteers on all shifts. Don't overlook staff such as chaplains and patient care volunteers.

- Audit the hospital's personnel records for all levels and disciplines to verify that competencies have been defined for each job.

- Make a list of people with hands-on duties and determine what skills and expectations are required to carry out each job. Problem-prone, high-risk, and infrequently used skills are particularly appropriate areas for competence assessment. Start with a job description and highlight functions that the employee performs most frequently and are the highest-risk activities. Select a few competencies for each job as a starting place and think about what skills, knowledge, and attitudes the individual needs to succeed in each of these areas.

- Involve the staff in defining the skills required for the job.

- Review agency contracts and ensure that all agency personnel have defined competence requirements and that the agency assesses competence initially and on a continual basis. Ensure that each contract specifically states that the organization under contract will meet JCAHO requirements and state and federal regulations.

Sidebar 2-3

The Survey of Information Related to Contracted Personnel and Volunteer Staff

Surveyors will ask the hospital being surveyed if it uses contracted personnel or volunteers for patient care and/or services. If so, hospital staff should present copies of the hospital's policies and procedures that demonstrate compliance with the Human Resource standards for contracted and volunteer personnel.

The surveyor may choose to review personnel files or the appropriate information for contract and volunteer personnel. The hospital does not need to keep the information on contracted personnel in the hospital. It need only make it available to the surveyor upon request. Acceptable methods could include the following:

- Having the personnel, health and education records brought to the surveyor during the survey;

- The surveyor's going to the contracted organization, or meeting with the contracted individual to review the information during the survey, if time permits; and

- Having the contracted organization, agency, or individual fax excerpts of the required information during the survey.

Who Is Qualified to Assess Competence?

Those who assess competence must be qualified to do so. Some small hospitals have trouble assessing staff when only one individual performs a specific function (for example, a small hospital with only one social worker). Hospitals that are part of a system may be able to use equivalent staff members from other facilities to perform reciprocal assessments. A social worker can assess another social worker, a therapist can assess another therapist, and so forth. However, their jobs must be similar in terms of the competencies required to meet the special needs and behaviors of specific patient age groups served by the hospital. For example, a case manager working with individuals who have developmental disabilities should be assessed by another professional in this area, rather than by a case manager who works with individuals with drug dependencies. To ensure that qualified personnel perform the competence assessment, hospitals should

- Define the qualifications of persons performing assessments for each type of staff member.
- Identify and make arrangements for reciprocal assessments with qualified staff at nearby hospitals in instances in which only one individual performs a specific function.
- Use staff within the organization to assess a more general skills demonstration (such as infection control procedures), perform a record review for communication skills, and verify education and licensure.

A hospital's vigilance in ensuring initial competence of all staff who provide care or services for the hospital is critical to patient safety. Competence must be maintained through an equally vigilant continuing competence assessment process—the subject of Chapter 3.

REFERENCES

1. Esque TJ, Gilbert TF: Making competencies pay off. *Training* Jan 1995, pp. 16–19.
2. Decker PJ: The hidden competencies of healthcare: Why self-esteem, accountability, and professionalism may affect hospital customer satisfaction scores. *Hosp Topics* 77(1): 14–26, Winter 1999.
3. Decker PJ, Strader MK, and Wise RJ: Beyond JCAHO: Using competency models to improve healthcare organizations, Part 2: Developing competence assessment systems. *Hosp Topics* 75(2): 10–17, Spring 1997.
4. National Institutes of Health Office of Human Resources Management, Clinical Center Education & Training: Competency. <*http://ohrm.cc.nih.gov/train/competency/core-comp.html*> (accessed Jan 14, 2002).
5. Martin AE, Stumpf JL, and Ryan ML: Assessing pharmacists' competence in clinical information retrieval. *Am J Health-Syst Pharm* 53:2957–2958, Dec 15, 1996.
6. Wolcoff M: *Cross Cultural Communication.* Anchorage, Alaska: Association of Stranded Rural Alaskans, 1987.
7. Turk DC: Pain assessment. Presented at the 2001 Joint Commission Leadership Summit on Pain Management in Phoenix, Arizona, Jun 25-26, 2001.
8. Ray A: Assessment of Pain Panel Presentation. Presented at the 2001 Joint Commission Leadership Summit on Pain Management in Phoenix, Arizona, Jun 25-26, 2001.
9. Wick JY, Zanni GR: Cultural competence: A pragmatic plan for fulfilling a professional imperative. *The Consultant Pharmacist* 16(3): 197–211, Mar 2001.
10. Berger JT: Culture and ethnicity in clinical care. *Arch Intern Med* 158:2085–2095, 1998.
11. Huffman M: Competency-based orientation for perioperative cardiovascular nurses. *AORN Journal* 61(4): 722–729, Apr 1995.
12. O'Grady T, O'Brien A: A guide to competency-based orientation. *J Nurs Staff Development,* May/June 1992, pp. 128–133.
13. Competency assessment begins at orientation. *Same-Day Surgery* Apr 2000, pps. 44–45.
14. Boylan CR, Westra R: Meeting Joint Commission requirements for staff nurse competency. *J Nurs Care Qual* 12(4): 44–48, Apr 1998.
15. Bastable, S: *Nurse as Educator: Principles of Teaching and Learning.* Sudbury, MA: Jones and Bartlett, 1997. Cited in McConnell EA: Competence vs. competency. *Nurs Manage* 32(5): 14, May 2001.
16. Spencer LM, and Spencer SM: *Competence at Work.* New York: John Wiley & Sons, 1993.

Example 2-1

Sample (Chief) Privacy Officer Job Description

Position Title: (Chief) Privacy Officer[1]

Immediate Supervisor: Chief Executive Officer, Senior Executive, or Health Information Management (HIM) Department Head[2]

General Purpose: The privacy officer oversees all ongoing activities related to the development, implementation, maintenance of, and adherence to the organization's policies and procedures covering the privacy of, and access to, patient health information in compliance with federal and state laws and the healthcare organization's information privacy practices.

Responsibilities:

- Provides development guidance and assists in the identification, implementation, and maintenance of organization information privacy policies and procedures in coordination with organization management and administration, the Privacy Oversight Committee,[3] and legal counsel.

- Works with organization senior management and corporate compliance officer to establish an organization-wide Privacy Oversight Committee.

- Serves in a leadership role for the Privacy Oversight Committee's activities.

- Performs initial and periodic information privacy risk assessments and conducts related ongoing compliance monitoring activities in coordination with the entity's other compliance and operational assessment functions.

- Works with legal counsel and management, key departments, and committees to ensure the organization has and maintains appropriate privacy and confidentiality consent, authorization forms, and information notices and materials reflecting current organization and legal practices and requirements.

- Oversees, directs, delivers, or ensures delivery of initial and privacy training and orientation to all employees, volunteers, medical and professional staff, contractors, alliances, business associates, and other appropriate third parties.

- Participates in the development, implementation, and ongoing compliance monitoring of all trading partner and business associate agreements, to ensure all privacy concerns, requirements, and responsibilities are addressed.

- Establishes with management and operations a mechanism to track access to protected health information, within the purview of the organization and as required by law and to allow qualified individuals to review or receive a report on such activity.

(continued on next page)

SOURCE: American Health Information Management Association. Used with permission.

Sample (Chief) Privacy Officer Job Description (continued)

- Works cooperatively with the HIM Director and other applicable organization units in overseeing patient rights to inspect, amend, and restrict access to protected health information when appropriate.

- Establishes and administers a process for receiving, documenting, tracking, investigating, and taking action on all complaints concerning the organization's privacy policies and procedures in coordination and collaboration with other similar functions and, when necessary, legal counsel.

- Ensures compliance with privacy practices and consistent application of sanctions for failure to comply with privacy policies for all individuals in the organization's workforce, extended workforce, and for all business associates, in cooperation with Human Resources, the information security officer, administration, and legal counsel as applicable.

- Initiates, facilitates and promotes activities to foster information privacy awareness within the organization and related entities.

- Serves as a member of, or liaison to, the organization's IRB or Privacy Committee,[4] should one exist. Also serves as the information privacy liaison for users of clinical and administrative systems.

- Reviews all system-related information security plans throughout the organization's network to ensure alignment between security and privacy practices, and acts as a liaison to the information systems department.

- Works with all organization personnel involved with any aspect of release of protected health information, to ensure full coordination and cooperation under the organization's policies and procedures and legal requirements

- Maintains current knowledge of applicable federal and state privacy laws and accreditation standards, and monitors advancements in information privacy technologies to ensure organizational adaptation and compliance.

- Serves as information privacy consultant to the organization for all departments and appropriate entities.

- Cooperates with the Office of Civil Rights, other legal entities, and organization officers in any compliance reviews or investigations.

- Works with organization administration, legal counsel, and other related parties to represent the organization's information privacy interests with external parties (state or local government bodies) who undertake to adopt or amend privacy legislation, regulation, or standard.

Qualifications:

- Certification as an RHIA or RHIT with education and experience relative to the size and scope of the organization.

(continued on next page)

SOURCE: American Health Information Management Association. Used with permission.

Sample (Chief) Privacy Officer Job Description (continued)

- Knowledge and experience in information privacy laws, access, release of information, and release control technologies.

- Knowledge in and the ability to apply the principles of HIM, project management, and change management.

- Demonstrated organization, facilitation, communication, and presentation skills.

This description is intended to serve as a scalable framework for organizations in development of a position description for the privacy officer.

Notes

1. The title for this position will vary from organization to organization, and may not be the primary title of the individual serving in the position. "Chief" would most likely refer to very large integrated delivery systems. The term "privacy officer" is specifically mention in the HIPAA Privacy Regulation.

2. Again, the supervisor for this position will vary depending on the institution and its size. Since many of the functions are already inherent in the Health Information or Medical Records Department or function, many organizations may elect to keep this function in that department.

3. The "Privacy Oversight Committee" described here is a recommendation of AHIMA, and should not be considered the same as the "Privacy Committee" described in the HIPAA privacy regulation. A privacy oversight committee could include representation from the organization's senior administration, in addition to departments and individuals who can lend an organization-wide perspective to privacy implementation and compliance.

4. Not all organizations will have an Institutional Review Board (IRB) or Privacy Committee for oversight of research activities. However, should such bodies be present or require establishment under HIPAA or other federal or state requirements, the privacy officer will need to work with this group(s) to ensure authorizations and awareness are established where needed or required.

SOURCE: American Health Information Management Association. Used with permission.

Example 2-2

Job Description for OR Staff Nurse

Rockingham Memorial Hospital
Job Description / Performance Appraisal and Competency Evaluation (PACE Form)

Position Title	OR Staff Nurse	Employee Name	
Department	OR	Supervisor	Squad Leader
Position Code:		Created Date: 11/01 Revised Date(s):10/00;2/99;9/92;5/90	
HR Review & Approval: _____/_____ Initials/Date		Dept Review & Approval: _____/_____ Initials/Date	

Our Mission, Vision, and Values

Our **Mission** is to be an innovative community-oriented health care provider committed to offering accessible, personalized, and high-quality services in a cost-effective manner.
Our **Vision** is to be the provider of choice in the market we serve.
Our **Core Values** are: Service * Enthusiasm * Respect * Value * Integrity * Communication * Excellence

I. Overview of Job
Basic Purpose of Position

Responsible for the supervision/delivery of perioperative care to patients from pediatrics through the life span using the nursing process.

Contacts

Supervises:	Has no supervisory responsibility # Direct Reports: _____ # Indirect Reports: LPN's, ORT's, OR Patient Care Assistants, Unit Secretaries.
Age of Patient Populations Served:	❏ Infant: Birth <1 yr ❏ Adolescents: 13 <18 yrs ❏ Toddler: < 2 1/2 yrs ❏ Adults: 18 < 65 yrs ❏ Pre-School: 2 - <4 1/2 yrs ❏ Older Adult: 65+ ❏ School Age: 4 1/2 < 13 yrs XX All ❏ Not applicable
Internal Contacts	❏ Patients ❏ Providers: (i.e. Physicians, Therapists, Social Workers) ❏ Staff: (i.e. clinical and administrative support staff)
External Contacts	❏ Outpatients ❏ Vendors ❏ Community Health Agencies and Advocates ❏ Other _____

(continued on next page)

EXAMPLES

EXAMPLES

Job Description for OR Staff Nurse (continued)

Overtime Status	
Overtime Status	❑ Exempt - "Salaried" Employee not eligible for overtime. XX Non-Exempt - "Hourly" Employee eligible for overtime. **If eligible for overtime,** Employee will be paid time and one-half for time worked: ❑ Over 40 hours per week, or ❑ Over 8 hours each day, and over 80 hours in the two week pay period.

Job Requirements

Minimum Education
Graduate of NLN approved RN education program.

Minimum Work Experience
None required; med/surg experience preferred.

Required Licenses
Current licensure as a registered nurse from the Virginia State Board of Nursing. Currently qualified in BCLS.

Workplace Conditions

Physical Requirements / Environmental Conditions
Position patients; may require lifting up to 90 lbs using correct lifting techniques. Frequent exposure to chemicals in OR (please see MSDS).

Blood-borne Pathogen Exposure Category

Category # I

Category I   Job usually involves contact with patients or patient specimens. Exposure to blood, body fluids, non-intact skin or tissue specimens, is possible.

Category II   Job may expose incumbent occasionally or in emergency situations to blood, body fluids, non-intact skin or tissue specimens.

Category III   Job does not involve exposure to blood, body fluids, non-intact skin or tissue specimens. Incumbent does not perform or help in emergency medical care or first aid as a part of his/her job.

(continued on next page)

EXAMPLES

Job Description for OR Staff Nurse (continued)

II. Organizational Competencies

The following section relates to the Core Values of RMH and contains standards for which all Employees, regardless of their position within the organization, are accountable.

1. Service
❏ Exceeds (Criteria are listed for each level of performance.)
❏ Meets
❏ Does Not Meet

2. Enthusiasm
❏ Exceeds
❏ Meets
❏ Does Not Meet

3. Respect
❏ Exceeds
❏ Meets
❏ Does Not Meet

4. Value
❏ Exceeds
❏ Meets
❏ Does Not Meet

5. Integrity
❏ Exceeds
❏ Meets
❏ Does Not Meet

6. Communication
❏ Exceeds
❏ Meets
❏ Does Not Meet

7. Excellence
❏ Exceeds
❏ Meets
❏ Does Not Meet

8. Confidentiality
❏ Exceeds
❏ Meets
❏ Does Not Meet

9. Attendance and Punctuality
❏ Exceeds
❏ Meets
❏ Does Not Meet

(continued on next page)

Job Description for OR Staff Nurse (continued)

IIa. Clinical Competencies
The following section relates to the Core Clinical Competencies for RMH and contains standards for which employees in all clinical departments are accountable.

1. Abuse and Neglect   ❑ *Not Applicable to this Position*
❑ Exceeds (Criteria are listed for each level of performance.)
❑ Meets
❑ Does not meet

2. Standard Precautions and Infection Control   ❑ *Not Applicable to this Position*
❑ Exceeds
❑ Meets
❑ Does Not Meet

3. Pain Management   ❑ *Not Applicable to this Position*
❑ Exceeds
❑ Meets
❑ Does Not Meet

4. Patient Safety   ❑ *Not Applicable to this Position*
❑ Exceeds
❑ Meets
❑ Does not Meet

5. Restraints & Seclusion   ❑ *Not Applicable to this Position*
❑ Exceeds
❑ Meets
❑ Does Not Meet

6. Emergency Preparedness   ❑ *Not Applicable to this Position*
❑ Exceeds
❑ Meets
❑ Does Not Meet

Organizational Competency Summary and Action Plan

Based on the above, list personal/professional development strategies and goals that will further enhance this individual's level of competency:
_____
_____
_____

❑ No specific action needed at this time.
❑ Formal Individual Performance Improvement Plan is needed. (See attached)

(continued on next page)

EXAMPLES

EXAMPLES

Job Description for OR Staff Nurse (continued)

III. Key Results and Standards of Performance

*In this section, Key Result Areas and Standards of Performance are defined. In order to receive a **Meets** rating, all of the standards within that area must be met. To achieve an **Exceeds** rating, all of the Meets and 50% of all of the Exceeds Standards must be met.*

1. Assessment	5% of time
❏ Exceeds	❏ Acts as a role model and mentor in assessment skills, consistently identifies subtleties in patient condition. Always follows through. ❏ Makes recommendations for quality improvement/special projects/initiatives. Sees through approval and implementation stages.
❏ Meets	❏ Performs preop assessment according to established policies and procedures. ❏ Accurately assesses safety level of patients, physical, social, mental status, cultural needs. Verifies surgical site, consent forms, etc.
❏ Does Not Meet	❏ Assessment contains information that is inaccurate, sketchy, and/or not timely as observed by Supervisor/peers/health care team. ❏ Lacks clinical knowledge to perform assessment.
Comments are required to justify an Exceeds/Does Not Meet rating.	

2. Planning and Implementation	70% of time
❏ Exceeds	❏ Functions effectively and competently in all surgeries, as per feedback and observation.
❏ Meets	❏ Functions effectively as a circulating RN. Plans, directs, provides and supervises perioperative care of the surgical patients of all ages. ❏ Functions in the roles of first and second assistant, working within the sterile field for the duration of the case or relief. ❏ When functioning as a first assistant, demonstrates solid knowledge of anatomy and physiology. ❏ When functioning as a second assistant, demonstrates solid knowledge of instrumentation and established protocol. ❏ Lifts and/or moves heavy equipment/supplies in the preparation, management and cleanup of surgical procedures.
❏ Does Not Meet	❏ Does not follow established procedures on more than one occasion during the evaluation period. ❏ Fails to individualize treatment plan.
Comments are required to justify an Exceeds/Does Not Meet rating.	

(continued on next page)

Job Description for OR Staff Nurse (continued)

3. Education and Teaching		5% of time
❑ Exceeds	❑ Recommends new and improved nursing/cost containment/quality improvement initiatives based on current professional literature. Sees through approval and implementation stages. ❑ Presents at least one in-service to staff on new, difficult, or infrequently performed procedures.	
❑ Meets	❑ Identifies learning needs of unit personnel and students to provide for optimal clinical practice. ❑ Assists new staff members/students with procedures and/or unit orientation.	
❑ Does Not Meet	❑ Not helpful on more than one occasion during the evaluation period.	
Comments are required to justify an Exceeds/Does Not Meet rating.		

4. Documentation		10% of time
❑ Exceeds	❑ Makes recommendations for quality improvement/special projects/initiatives. Sees through approval and implementation stages.	
❑ Meets	❑ Documentation is complete, legible and timely. ❑ Appropriate forms are utilized and complete.	
❑ Does Not Meet	❑ Supervisor has had to counsel employee on more than three occasions during the evaluation period regarding incomplete documentation.	
Comments are required to justify an Exceeds/Does Not Meet rating.		

5. Medication Administration		5% of time
❑ Exceeds	❑ Stays current on medication administration knowledge. ❑ Functions as department resource on medication knowledge.	
❑ Meets	❑ Demonstrates competency in all medication administration and blood product transfusion.	
❑ Does Not Meet	❑ Supervisor has had to counsel employee on more than one occasion during the evaluation period regarding incomplete documentation.	
Comments are required to justify an Exceeds/Does Not Meet rating.		

(continued on next page)

EXAMPLES

Job Description for OR Staff Nurse (continued)

6. Departmental Policies and Procedures	5% of time
❏ Exceeds	❏ Makes recommendations for staff education, in-services and quality improvement of RMH. Sees through approval and implementation stages.
❏ Meets	❏ Always attends required in-services, and actively participates in self-education. ❏ Completes all job functions as per departmental policies and procedures.
❏ Does Not Meet	❏ Employee has missed one mandatory in-service during the evaluation period. Supervisor has had to counsel more than two times during the evaluation period with regard to following policies and procedures.
Comments are required to justify an Exceeds/Does Not Meet rating.	

Key Results and Standards Summary and Action Plan

Based on the above, list personal/professional development strategies and goals that will further enhance this individual's level of performance:

_____
_____
_____

❏ No specific action needed at this time.
❏ Formal Individual Performance Improvement Plan is needed. (See attached)

(continued on next page)

Job Description for OR Staff Nurse (continued)

EXAMPLES

IV. Job Specific Competencies
Job Specific Competencies are skills that are needed to successfully perform in this position.

COMPETENCY	TYPE	AGE OF PATIENT POPULATION SERVED	COMPETENCY CONTINUUM LEVEL	METHOD OF ASSESSMENT	ASSESSOR
Aseptic technique Patient safety **CLIN**	High volume	☐ Infant: Birth<1 yr ☐ Toddler: 1<2 1/2 yrs ☐ Pre-School: 2 1/2<4 1/2 yrs ☐ School Age: 4 1/2<13 yrs ☐ Adolescents: 13 18 yrs ☐ Adults: 18<65 yrs ☐ Older Adult: 65+ ☐ All ☐ Not applicable	☐ 1 ☐ 2 Developing ☐ 3 ☐ 4 Proficient ☐ 5 ☐ 6 Advanced	☐ Observed ☐ Demonstrated ☐ Verbalized ☐ Test	_____/_____ Initials/Date
Malignant hyperthermia **CLIN**	Low Vol/ High Risk	☐ Infant: Birth <1 yr ☐ Toddler: 1<2 1/2 yrs ☐ Pre-School: 2 1/2<4 1/2 yrs ☐ School Age: 4 1/2<13 yrs ☐ Adolescents: 1318 yrs ☐ Adults: 18<65 yrs ☐ Older Adult: 65+ ☐ All ☐ Not applicable	☐ 1 ☐ 2 Developing ☐ 3 ☐ 4 Proficient ☐ 5 ☐ 6 Advanced	☐ Observed ☐ Demonstrated ☐ Verbalized ☐ Test	_____/_____ Initials/Date
New Instruments/ equipment **EQUIP** Computers and software **COMP**	New technology	☐ Infant: Birth <1 yr ☐ Toddler: 1<2 1/2 yrs ☐ Pre-School: 2 1/2<4 1/2 yrs ☐ School Age: 4 1/2<13 yrs ☐ Adolescents: 1318 yrs ☐ Adults: 18<65 yrs ☐ Older Adult: 65+ ☐ All ☐ Not applicable	☐ 1 ☐ 2 Developing ☐ 3 ☐ 4 Proficient ☐ 5 ☐ 6 Advanced	☐ Observed ☐ Demonstrated ☐ Verbalized ☐ Test	_____/_____ Initials/Date

The Competency Continuum

LEVEL	#	STAGE	DESCRIPTION
Developing	1 2	Learning Exhibiting	Minimum level of competency Some command of competency
Proficient	3 4	Demonstrating Modeling	Consistent command of competency Best example of competency
Advanced	5 6	Teaching Leading	Instructs others in competency Innovates, advances competency

(continued on next page)

Job Description for OR Staff Nurse (continued)

Methods of Assessment Definitions

Observed Assessor has watched skill being performed in actual practice.
Verbalized Employee has verbally demonstrated sufficient knowledge and competency of skill.
Demonstrated Assessor has watched employee demonstrate or present this skill.
Test An objective test measuring this competency was successfully completed.

Competency Classifications

ADMIN Administrative
CLIN Technical: Clinical
COMP Technical: Computer/Software
CORE Clinical Core Competencies
CSVS Customer Service

EQUIP Equipment/Mechanical
MGMT Management/Leadership
PERS Interpersonal Skills
PROF Professional/ Trade Knowledge
OTHER Other

Job Specific Competencies Summary and Action Plan

Based on the above, list personal/professional development strategies and goals that will further enhance this individual's level of job specific competency:

_____
_____
_____
_____

❏ No specific action needed at this time.
❏ Formal Individual Performance Improvement Plan is needed. (See attached)

(continued on next page)

Job Description for OR Staff Nurse (continued)

V. Performance Score

Performance Rating Levels
4 = Exceeds rating   2 = Meets rating   0 = Does not meet rating

Key Result Areas (90%)

	Key Result Area	Performance Rating Level		Weight	Score
1. Enter the appropriate Performance Rating Level and weight for each Key Result Area.	1.		X		=
	2.		X		=
	3.		X		=
	4.		X		=
2. Multiply the Performance Level Rating times the weight.	5.		X		=
	6.		X		=
	7.		X		=
3. Total the score column.	8.		X		=
	9.		X		=
				100%	

Total for Key Results [   ]

Organizational Competencies (10%)

	Key Result Area	Performance Rating Level		Weight	Score
	Competency		X	10%	=
1. Circle the Performance Rating Level for each competency.	Service		X	10%	=
	Enthusiasm		X	10%	=
	Respect		X	10%	=
2. Enter the result in the score column.	Value		X	10%	=
	Integrity		X	10%	=
	Communication		X	10%	=
3. Total the score column.	Excellence		X	10%	=
	Confidentiality		X	20%	=
	Attendance/Punctuality		X	10%	=
				100%	

Total for Organizational Competencies [   ]

Total Score

1. Copy the totals for Key Result and Competency scores from shaded boxes above.
2. Multiply times the rating to get the weighted score.
3. Add the weighted score to get the Total Score.

SCORE From above

Key Result Score [   ] X 90% = [   ]
(A)

Organizational Competency Score [   ] X 10% = [   ]
(B)

Total Score [   ]
(A+B)

(continued on next page)

EXAMPLES

EXAMPLES

Job Description for OR Staff Nurse (continued)

VI. Overall Summary

Annual Performance Appraisal and Competency Evaluation

Additional Supervisor Comments: (please use extra pages if necessary)

Employee Comments: (please use extra pages if necessary)

VII. Employee Statement of Understanding, Confidentiality, and Compliance

I agree to uphold the Mission, Vision, and Values; **S**ervice * **E**nthusiasm * **R**espect * **V**alue * **I**ntegrity * **C**ommunication * **E**xcellence, of Rockingham Memorial Hospital.

I understand that this document is intended to describe the general nature and level of work being performed. The statements in this document are not intended to be construed as an exhaustive list of all responsibilities, duties and skills required of personnel so classified.

Rockingham Memorial Hospital is committed to protecting the confidentiality of information concerning Patients, Employees, and Facility Operations. Furthermore, we are committed to protecting the interests of our patients, community, and organization by ensuring that we consistently provide the highest quality health care services at the most affordable cost.

I agree that, as an Employee of Rockingham Memorial Hospital, I have a legal and moral responsibility to protect the confidentiality of privileged information obtained by me through the delivery of patient care and/or daily facility operations, and I agree not to share or release personal health information or other confidential information to anyone who does not have a right or need to know.

I understand that the improper communication of confidential information (i.e., the release, possession, copying, use, reading or discussion of such information inappropriately or without proper authority) is strictly prohibited and considered grounds for disciplinary action up to and including termination of employment.

Confidential information includes facts, anecdotes, data, perceptions and other knowledge of patients, employees, physicians, patient care providers and other organizational business obtained in the work environment. This includes, but is not limited to, information learned from verbal, written, computerized, faxed, emailed, audio or video taped, observed, or other means.

I understand my responsibility to follow the Hospital's guidelines as stated in the Confidentiality/ Information Access policy. The policy is found in the Hospital Policy Manual, and is available to all departments and units. I understand the Hospital will take disciplinary action against anyone who does not follow these established guidelines.

It is the responsibility of all Employees and members of the Medical Staff to make certain that RMH services are provided in an ethical, legal, and compliant manner and to disclose to management any violation or potential violation of RMH's Code of Conduct. I understand that failure to report fraudulent behavior will result in disciplinary action up to and including termination of employment.

Currently, I am aware of no unreported issue that could pose a risk of non-compliance to RMH. If I am or do become aware of any activity that could pose a risk of non-compliance and/or may violate RMH's Code of Conduct, I will notify management or the Compliance Hotline immediately.

Employee Signature: _____ **Date:** _____

Print your name: _____

Supervisor Signature: _____ **Date:** _____

_____ **Date:** _____

Example 2-3

Adult and Geriatric Characteristics and Competency Expectations

Stage	Age	Behavior or Need	Competency Expectation
General Adult	19 to Death	Ensure an environment that provides privacy and maintains confidentiality. Involve patient in all aspects of care including decision-making, informed consent and mutuality in the development of the plan of care. Involve family/significant other as appropriate. Individual plan of care taking into consideration the patient's past experience, needs and goals.	Accepts adult's chosen life-style and adjustments relating to health status. Communicates in a respectful manner. Provides information and instruction at a level of understanding appropriate to the comprehension level of the patient and/or family. Provides teaching based on readiness to learn.
Young Adult	20 to 40 years	Life is goal directed with a personal family life and job responsibilities usually evolving or established. Stage of development is intimacy vs. isolation. Young adult is developing a sense of identity and is moving toward establishing an intimate relationship with another person. Impact of illness has a direct effect on spouse/significant other, children and aging parent responsibilities and relationships. Reaction to illness/health change may include fear, guilt, denial and/or defensiveness. The plan of care is based on knowledge of home conditions, occupational considerations and religious/cultural background and needs.	Recognizes person's commitments and the function of competency in life. Supports change as necessary for health and the patient's right to make informed choices. Incorporates person's life situations, home environment, responsibilities and available resources into plan of care. Assists person in coping and problem solving related to current situation.
Middle Adulthood	40 to 65 years	Life style is established with specific, definite goals. Stage of development is generativity vs. stagnation; parenting and involvement with family and life situations of primary importance. Affect of illness/condition and reaction has same impact as with young adult, with the realization of aging and health changes having longer lasting impact on relationships and productivity. The plan of care continues to be based on knowledge of home situations, occupational considerations and religious/cultural background and needs.	Provides care and respect the same as to young adult. Assists person to plan for anticipated change in life style or situation. Assists person to recognize the risk factors related to health, and to focus on strengths rather than weaknesses.

(continued on next page)

SOURCE: Upper Chesapeake Health–Harford Memorial Hospital. Used with permission of Upper Chesapeake Health–Harford Memorial Hospital, MD.

EXAMPLES

EXAMPLES

Adult and Geriatric Characteristics and Competency Expectations (continued)

Stage	Age	Behavior or Need	Competency Expectation
Geriatric - Older Adult	65–75 years	Support system and recent changes in life may have a bearing on ability to meet personal needs. Physical changes may affect sight, hearing and strength. Needs to continue activities and contacts with peer group. May require increased awareness of safety and environmental needs. The plan of care is based on knowledge of home conditions, available resources and religious/cultural background and needs.	Ensures communication in a manner that meets the person's physical abilities, i.e sight and hearing needs. Promotes self-care and encourages support from family, friends and clergy. Assists in keeping physically and socially active. Works to encourage and maintain peer group interactions. Promotes positive feeling about aging through respectful communication and interactions. Promotes health through education of the normal aging changes. Fosters independence through adapting the environment to facilitate maximal functioning. Involves patient in plan of care; involves family/significant other as appropriate or necessary. Supports patient through periods on anxiety by allowing discussion and listening to expressions of troubles and difficulties. Acts as an advocate for identified problems and contacts/provides resources to meet psychosocial needs of the patient and/or family.
Geriatric - Elderly	75 and older	Physiological and psychosocial changes affect the elderly person and his/her family. Functional capacities change, including strength, sensory, emotional and communication alterations. External components, such as living arrangement, financial resources, personal network of family, friend and peer group as well as available services impact on the lifestyle of the older adult and elderly person. The stage of development is ego integrity vs. despair; the individual is reflecting on and accepting one's life and/or dealing with unmet goals and family/friend losses. The plan of care is based on knowledge of home/living environment, provision of a safe environment, religious/cultural background and needs, and special needs related to aging process.	Takes into account the physiological and psychological changes occurring in the aging process. Assists patient with self-care as required, maintaining as much independence as possible. Ensures care that is respectful of age and changes in abilities and sensorium. Includes patient in care decisions and participation in care activities. Communicates in a respectful and caring manner to maintain the dignity of the individual. Takes time to listen when the person indicates an interest or need to discuss issues such as questions/concerns, loss of loved one(s) or process of own death. Listens and communicates taking into account the life experience of the patient and their personal decisions non-judgementally. Provides care and therapies in a manner that takes into account the special needs of the patient.

Example 2-4

Radiology Age-Specific Competency

River Parishes Hospital

RADIOLOGY AGE SPECIFIC COMPETENCY

NAME:_____   Position:_____
Instructor:_____   Date:_____

Legend: B.O. = Behavior Observed
               R.D. = Return Demonstration

NEONATE (1 – 28 DAYS)

                                                          YES   NO
Should remain covered with a blanket to conserve body heat.
Calls for emergency procedures should be responded to immediately.
Collimate to a specific area. Shield patient and parent / attendant.
Exposure times should be as short as possible to eliminate motion.
Cover cassette and shield with a baby blanket to protect skin from abrasions and coldness
     of the cassette.
If parents are present, explain procedure to them.
If possible, involve parents in procedure.
Never leave patient unattended on x-ray table.

INFANT (29 days – 2 years)

                                                          YES   NO
Collimate to a specific area. Shield patient and parent / attendant. Always shield
     reproductive organs.
Exposure times should be as short as possible to eliminate motion.
If necessary, use positioning aids.
If parents are present, explain procedure to them.
If possible, involve parents in procedure.
Cover cassette and shield with a baby blanket to protect skin from abrasions and coldness
     of the cassette.
Never leave patient unattended on x-ray table.

CHILD (3 – 12 years)

                                                          YES   NO
Collimate to a specific area. Shield patient and parent / attendant. Always shield
     reproductive organs.
Exposure times should be as short as possible to eliminate motion.
If necessary, use positioning aids.
If parents are present, explain procedure to them.
If possible, involve parents in procedure.

(continued on next page)

EXAMPLES

EXAMPLES

Radiology Age-Specific Competency (continued)

Contrast medium is administered by Radiologist or Technologist in dosage prescribed by
   Radiologist following established protocols.
Explain and demonstrate equipment first.
Use distraction techniques.
Give child one direction at a time.
Speak at eye level with child; maintain eye contact. Use firm, direct approach.
Provide for privacy.
Never leave patient unattended on x-ray table.

ADOLESCENT (13–17 years)

                                                                    YES   NO

Collimate to a specific area. Shield patient and parent / attendant. Always shield
   reproductive organs.
All females of child-bearing age must be asked when last period was and whether any
   chance of being pregnant.
If necessary, use positioning aids.
Explain procedure to patient using correct terminology.
Involve parents in education about exam.
Allow child to exercise some control.
Explain and demonstrate equipment first.
Encourage questions regarding fears.
Contrast medium is administered by Radiologist or Technologist in dosage prescribed by
   Radiologist following established protocols.
Involve patient in decision-making and planning.
Provide for privacy.
Never leave patient unattended on x-ray table.

ADULT (18 – 69 years)

                                                                    YES   NO

Collimate to a specific area. Shield patient and parent / attendant. Always shield
   reproductive organs.
All females of child-bearing age must be asked when last period was and whether any
   chance of being pregnant.
If necessary, use positioning aids.
Provide education regarding procedure to patient and / or significant other.
Explain equipment used.
Involve patient in decision-making and planning.
Address patient using last name.
Provide for mobility.
Contrast medium is administered by Radiologist or Technologist in dosage prescribed by
   Radiologist following established protocols.
Never leave patient unattended on x-ray table.

(continued on next page)

Radiology Age-Specific Competency (continued)

GERIATRIC (70 plus years)

                                                                  YES   NO

Collimate to a specific area. Shield patient and attendant.

If necessary, use positioning aids.

Provide education regarding procedure.

Speak distinctly. Do not raise voice unless you have determined patient is hard of
    hearing.

Provide adequate lighting.

If necessary, slow down pace of exam.

Change positions slowly due to decreased circulation.

Ensure patient warmth due to decreased heat regulation.

Address patient using last name.

Provide for mobility.

Contrast medium is administered by Radiologist or Technologist in dosage prescribed by
    Radiologist following established protocols.

Never leave patient unattended on x-ray table.

EXAMPLES

Example 2-5

Supplemental Employment Application for Recreational Therapy Staff

DEPARTMENT OF RECREATIONAL THERAPY
SUPPLEMENTAL EMPLOYMENT APPLICATION

Instructions -- Please type or print in ink all sections of this application and affix your signature where indicated. <u>Incomplete applications will not be processed.</u> If more space is needed for answers, please attach additional sheets to the application. **Please attach an official transcript(s).**

I.   **Requested Departmental Specialization**

☐Pediatrics   ☐Psychiatry
☐Burn Center   ☐Rehabilitation   ☐Transplants

II. **List licenses, (including drivers license) certifications and registrations which you currently hold. Include identification numbers and expiration dates (please attach a photo copy of each).**

_____

_____

III. **Please list intervention skills (e.g. stress management/relaxation) in which you have demonstrated competence to use as a treatment intervention with patients.**

_____

_____

_____

_____

_____

IV. **Please list the following information about your internship:**

	Course Prefix	Course Number	Course Credit
Course Title _____			
_____	___	___	___

Agency Internship Supervisor_____Title_____

Agency Name_____

Agency Address_____

City_____ State_____ Zip Code_____

Internship Performed from _____ to _____   _____ x_____ = _____

                                                                            No. of wks. Hrs/wk. Total hrs.

Setting/Type of Agency _____

Primary Population Served _____

Academic Internship Supervisor _____Title_____

(continued on next page)

Source: UNC Hospital, Chapel Hill, NC. Used with permission.

Supplemental Employment Application for Recreational Therapy Staff (continued)

2 of 4

V.   Has an employer ever formally disciplined (e.g. written warning, suspension, demotion, or termination) you for performance or conduct?

☐ No   ☐ Yes (Please explain below)

_____

_____

VI.   Have you ever been disciplined or sanctioned by a credentialling organization (e.g. North Carolina Therapeutic Recreation Certification Board, National Council for Therapeutic Recreation Certification, etc.)?

☐ No   ☐ Yes (Please explain below)

_____

_____

VII.   Please list all professional malpractice actions in which you have been named as a defendant. Indicate the nature of the allegations and the status or outcome of the action(s).

_____

_____

VIII.   Please list all professional organizations in which you are a member.

Organization   Expiration Date

_____

_____

_____

_____

IX.   <u>References</u>: Please list three references. No more than one may come from any one of following groups: Professor, Agency Administrator, Former Supervisor, Current Supervisor, Academic Peer, Professional Peer, Academic Advisor, Internship Supervisor.

1._____   2._____

_____   _____

_____   _____

3._____

_____

_____

(continued on next page)

EXAMPLES

EXAMPLES

Supplemental Employment Application for Recreational Therapy Staff
(continued)

3 of 4

UNC Hospitals Department of Recreational Therapy
Supplemental Employment Application
Competency Content Areas*

NAME _____

APPLICATION DATE _____

Content Area	Contact Time	Course Title	Course Prefix	Course No.	Course Credit
Therapeutic Recreation Content					
Foundations of Professional Practice	45 hr				
Assessment for Therapeutic Recreation	45 hr				
Therapeutic Recreation Intervention/ Program Planning	45 hr				
Leadership & Group Dynamics	45 hr				
Helping/Counseling Skills	45 hr				
Intervention Skills	___ hr				
Intervention Skills	___ hr				
Intervention Skills	___ hr				
Evaluation of TR Treatment Plan	45 hr				
Management of TR Services	45 hr				
Supportive Content					
Health Care Organization and Delivery	45 hr				
Legal Aspects of Health Care	45 hr				
Human Growth and Development	45 hr				
General Psychology	45 hr				
Education/Cognitive Psychology	45 hr				
Abnormal Psychology	45 hr				
Anatomy and Physiology	90 hr				
Kinesiology	45 hr				
Motor Skill Learning	45 hr				
Survey of Medical/Disabling Conditions	45 hr				
Pharmacology	30 hr				
Introduction to Recreation/Leisure Services	45 hr				

Consistent with certification requirements, the Department requires three therapeutic recreation content courses (*Note*: "Recreation For Special Populations" is **not** considered a therapeutic recreation content course).
* Source: American Therapeutic Recreation Association. (1997). *Guidelines for Competency Assessment and Curriculum Planning in Therapeutic Recreation: A Tool for Self Evaluation.* Hattiesburg, MS: ATRA.

(continued on next page)

Supplemental Employment Application for Recreational Therapy Staff (continued)

4 of 4

X.   Statement of Agency

UNC Hospitals will treat this application and any information secured in connection therewith in strict confidence, preserving with all reasonable safeguards the privacy of the applicant.   Only those persons involved in the employment process shall have access to this application and information secured in connection therewith.

XI.   Applicant's Agreements

I hereby authorize UNC Hospitals, the Department of Recreational Therapy and their representatives to consult with the references that I have listed, previous employers and representatives of academic institutions I have attended, to assess my professional competence, performance, professional ethics and ability to work with others.

I authorize representatives of UNC Hospitals to investigate my driving record in order to assess my competence and safety to transport patients.

If selected for a position with UNC Hospitals, I acknowledge that I will provide the highest level of care and supervision to my patients consistent with Hospitals' and Department of Recreational Therapy policies and procedures, standards of regulatory agencies, professional standards of practice and codes of ethics.

I agree to cooperatively participate in competency assessment activities and will successfully complete any courses or training deemed necessary by the Department of Recreational Therapy to enhance my competencies.

 I agree to maintain certification with the North Carolina Therapeutic Recreation Certification Board and the National Council for Therapeutic Recreation Certification. I understand that failure to maintain certification is just cause for termination.

I hereby release from liability all representatives of UNC Hospitals and the Department of Recreational Therapy staff for their acts performed in good faith and without malice in connection with evaluating my application, references, credentials and competence for employment. I also hereby release from liability all individuals and organizations who provide information, including otherwise privileged or confidential information, to UNC Hospitals or Department of Recreational Therapy staff in good faith and without malice concerning my professional qualifications, competence, performance, ethics and character and I hereby consent to the release of such information.

I certify that I have given true, accurate and complete information on this form. I understand that any false information contained herein or omissions may be grounds for rejection of my application or disciplinary action or dismissal if I am employed.

Signature_____Date_____

Revised 10/99

EXAMPLES

Example 2-6

Skills Self-assessment Inventory

**ALASKA NATIVE MEDICAL CENTER
NURSING SERVICE**

SKILLS SELF ASSESSMENT INVENTORY

PATIENT SERVICE ASSISTANT

_____   _____   ___/___/___
NAME **(PLEASE PRINT)**   UNIT   EOD

The objective of this skill sheet is to assist us in determining your current level of knowledge and experience in general nursing assistant skills. It is your responsibility to seek out opportunities to increase your experience and competency in these skills.

Please complete this skills sheet by **_initialing_** the column that best describes your current level of competence.

1. No contact with equipment or this patient situation. No knowledge of procedure.

2. Understand procedure and patient situation but never performed task.

3. Have performed this task infrequently and would need supervision.

4. Have performed this task frequently and can perform independently.

SKILL	1	2	3	4	COMMENTS
NEUROLOGICAL					
Seizure Precautions					
RESPIRATORY					
Turn, Cough and Deep Breathe					
CARDIOVASCULAR					
Basic Life Support					
Assessment of Vital Signs					
Blood Pressure					
Pulse					
Temperature					
Oral					

(continued on next page)

Source: Alaska Native Medical Center, Anchorage, AK. Used with permission.

Skills Self-assessment Inventory (continued)

SKILL	1	2	3	4	COMMENTS
Temperature (continued)					
Rectal					
Axillary					
Weight					
RENAL					
Measuring intake and output					
GASTROINTESTINAL					
Feeding patient					
Enemas					
ORTHOPEDIC					
Range of Motion Exercises:					
Passive					
Active					
Moving Patient					
Bed to wheelchair					
Wheelchair to bed					
Bed to bed					
Cast Care					
Hoyer Lift					
PATIENT HYGIENE					
Bath					
Tub					
Bed					
Shower					
Sitz					
Skin Care					
Dry					
Pressure areas					

(continued on next page)

EXAMPLES

Skills Self-assessment Inventory (continued)

SKILL	1	2	3	4	COMMENTS
Skin Care (cont.)					
Prevention of Decubitus					
Mouth Care					
Denture Care					
Hair Care					
COLLECTION OF SPECIMENS					
Stool					
Urine - clean catch					
Glucometer					
Sputum					
INFECTION CONTROL					
Universal precautions					
Respiratory isolation					
Clean dressing change					
MISCELLANEOUS					
Post-op Care					
Post Mortem Care					
Restraints					
Soft					
Leather					
Basic Charting Principles					
Phlebotomy					
Aeseptic Techniques					
Catheterization					
Insertion of catheter/catheter care					
Traction Set Up (Bucks traction)					
Feeding Tubes (Gastrostomy only)					
Suctioning					
Oropharyngeal					

(continued on next page)

Skills Self-assessment Inventory (continued)

SKILL	1	2	3	4	COMMENTS
Medical Terminology					
Order Transcription					
RPMS COMPUTER PACKAGE					
Computer Entry - RPMS					
Mailman					
Registration/admitting/discharge					
Scheduling Appointments					
Lab Order Entry					
Diet Order Entry					
Medication Profile					
Health Summary					
OTHER SKILLS (Unit Specific)					

I agree not to perform any skill rated less than 4 without supervision until I have developed competence in it.

_____   _____
EMPLOYEE SIGNATURE   DATE

I have received a copy of this Skills Inventory

_____   _____
NURSE MANAGER SIGNATURE   DATE

EXAMPLES

Example 2-7

Selected Practice Criteria for Cardiovascular Operating Room Nurses

Scope of practice: Provides nursing care for the patient undergoing surgery for cardiovascular disease (level 1)

Key function/ aspect of care	Performance criteria	Learning options	Evaluation methods	Date met and initials
Ensure a safe, therapeutic environment for the cardiac patient.	Complies with fire safety protocols.			
	a. Identifies location of fire alarms, exit doors, fire extinguishers, and oxygen shutoff valves (first day in cardiovascular OR).	Tour the OR with the preceptor.	Interview: return demonstration	_____
	b. Verbalizes actions to take in a fire.	Read safety standard for cardiac surgery. Locate and review hospital safety manual. Complete unit fire safety quiz. Watch video on fire safety.	Interview: objective quiz	_____
Maintain an aseptic environment.	Assists in draping the cardiac patient.	Read standard for draping. Observe demonstration by preceptor.	Return demonstration	_____
Provide continuity of care.	Demonstrates use of computer to document preoperative record, verify laboratory test results and blood type, and order laboratory tests and blood products.	Spend afternoon with preceptor/resource person to enter demonstration records in computer (first week in cardiovascular OR).	Return demonstration	_____

SOURCE: Huffman M: Competency-based orientation for perioperative cardiovascular nurses. *AORN Journal* 61(4): 722–729, Apr 1995. Used with permission. Copyright © AORN, Inc, 2170 S Parker Road, Suite 300, Denver, CO, 80231.

CHAPTER 3

Continuing Competence Assessment: Individuals Covered by Human Resources Standards

This chapter addresses continuing competence assessment for individuals covered by the Human Resources standards. It details how hospitals assess the competence of an individual from completion of the first review period through regular and continuing assessments at specified intervals.

The continuing competence assessment process includes the following four key activities:

- The department manager or appropriate staff member selects competencies to be evaluated on a continual basis, establishes the frequency of assessment, determines what methods will be used, and identifies the appropriate person to perform the assessment.
- The individual's supervisor or appropriate staff member assesses or validates the individual's competence in performing the identified competencies on a periodic basis.
- The hospital provides educational resources for the specific learning needs identified by the assessment process and provides training for any new equipment, new or revised processes used by the individual, or any competency issues identified through a review of quality data and indicators.
- The hospital collects and analyzes aggregate data on competence patterns and trends to identify and respond to learning needs.

A detailed description of each activity follows the discussion of JCAHO requirements related to these activities.

JCAHO Requirements

Hospital leaders are responsible for ensuring the continuing competence assessment of all individuals who work in the hospital by:

- seeing to it that the competence of all staff members is assessed, maintained, demonstrated, and continually improved;
- providing continuous in-service and other education and training to maintain and improve staff competence and support an interdisciplinary approach to patient care;
- regularly collecting data on competence patterns and trends to identify and respond to staff learning needs; and
- assessing each staff member's ability to meet the performance expectations set forth in his or her job description.

The Overview section of the Management of Human Resources chapter of the *Comprehensive Accreditation Manual for Hospitals: The Official Handbook (CAMH)* describes the role leaders play in assuring ongoing, periodic competence assessment that evaluates individuals' continuing abilities to perform throughout their association with the hospital. The intents of the standards describe how hospitals are required to collect and analyze aggregate data to assess staff competence and pinpoint training needs and to provide ongoing training to meet identified needs to improve staff competence.

Laying the Groundwork of a Continuing Process

Leaders establish the main components of a continuing competence assessment program or process. They determine

- what competencies must be assessed;
- when they should be assessed;
- how they should be assessed and by whom; and
- how they can be improved (that is, what resources will be needed for education and training to improve competence).

Hospitals can assess competence objectively in many ways, and individual hospitals can decide how to structure their competence assessment process. Such a process should meet the following criteria:

- the hospital uses a combination of continuing competence assessment and educational activities to maintain staff competence; and
- an objective, measurable system is used periodically to evaluate job performance, current competencies, and skills.

For hospital personnel hired through contractual arrangements, the hospital maintains a written job description and a completed competence assessment, evaluation, or appraisal tool for each such employee.

Identifying Competencies

After validating an individual's competence upon completion of the orientation process, the process of continuing competence assessment begins. Bonnie P. Britton, MSN, RN, Julia T. Raper, MSN, RN, and Christine M. Walden, MSN, RN, of University Medical Center of Eastern Carolina,

an expert team in competence assessment, note: "The competency criteria used to establish initial competency are also used to evaluate ongoing competency."[1] General and department or job-specific competencies must be identified along with the competencies required to meet the special needs and behaviors of specific patient age groups. Job-specific competencies focus on high-risk, low-volume, and/or problem-prone skills specific to the individual's job. Some competencies, such as universal precautions, should be defined as mandatory for all direct care providers, regardless of position.

On page 47 of Example 2-2, the multipurpose form used by Rockingham Memorial Hospital, the job-specific competencies that OR staff nurses must demonstrate are listed. Accompanying these competencies are levels of proficiency, the method of assessment, and a place for the assessor's initials and date of assessment.

Assessing Volunteers' Competencies. Competencies for volunteers should not be neglected. A close examination of each volunteer's job description is the starting point.

For example, job responsibilities of a volunteer who works at an information desk might include providing directions within the hospital to visitors and patients. The related competency could be defined as, "provides accurate directions to any location in the hospital," and evaluated via observation methods described later in this chapter. Two competencies for a volunteer who provides a snack service for patients might be defined as, "demonstrates ability to select age-appropriate snacks," and "demonstrates ability to perform the Heimlich maneuver."

Establishing the Frequency of Assessment

Leaders define how often an assessment needs to occur. This may vary, depending on the position, the patient population served, and law and regulation. Competence should be assessed at the time an individual is hired and after he or she receives orientation. Thereafter, the hospital determines the intervals for competence evaluation in accordance with organization policy and federal and state laws and regulations. JCAHO standards for continuing competence assessment state that assessment thereafter should occur "periodically." This means that the individual is reassessed according to applicable laws and regulations and the hospital's own policies and definitions. He or she is also assessed when given new job responsibilities, when the hospital institutes new procedures or techniques, and when new equipment or technology is introduced. Most hospitals require comprehensive performance evaluations that include competence assessment on an annual basis. Many also have organizationwide, department-specific, or unit-specific annual requirements.

Hospital leaders are responsible for defining policies regarding the evaluation of special skills. Determined by the frequency of use and risk factors, some skills may be evaluated every three or six months; others require evaluation every two years. In addition, the introduction of new medications, equipment, treatment interventions, or procedures may generate one-time qualification requirements or continuing, regular assessment. Leaders and department managers should determine what knowledge or skills are best assessed annually or more frequently and what can safely be assessed at longer intervals.

Determining Who Assesses Competence

Those who assess competence must be qualified to do so. This means that only an individual with the requisite expertise evaluates staff competence. This person may be an instructor, a preceptor, a supervisor, a peer with validated special skills, or a member of another discipline or department. For example, a psychiatric nurse clinical specialist is qualified to evaluate an RN's pediatric mental status assessment skills; a food service manager is qualified to evaluate a food service worker's knowledge and skills; a cardiopulmonary resuscitation (CPR) instructor is qualified to evaluate a nurse's resuscitation skills; and a respiratory therapist is qualified to evaluate a nurse's skills in managing the extubation of a patient. Members of another department might be qualified to assess general competencies. For example, an RN may be able to evaluate a therapist's competence in infection control procedures, care coordination, or patient education.

To assess the clinical competence of a large staff of emergency room nurses (defined as more than 90 registered nurses), for example, Robert W. Ready, RN, MN, CEN, clinical educator at Rhode Island Hospital in Providence, reports that the hospital identified potentially qualified observers or testers among nurse managers, assistant nurse managers, trauma coordinators, unit teachers, clinical educators, experienced nurses advanced on the clinical ladder, and nurses with master's degrees who had demonstrated mastery of required clinical skills within their area of specialty.[2] Those qualified to assess the competence of emergency room nurses had to meet two standards: ability to meet all test criteria and demonstrated ability to evaluate others. Problems occurred with the selection of nurse managers as testers for the following three reasons:

- their supervisory position contributed to the perception of a threatening testing environment;
- some managers lacked recent clinical experience; and
- some could not afford to take time away from their management responsibilities for testing.

In these instances, the use of non-managers provided an alternative.

Determining Assessment Methods

Numerous ways to assess competence exist. Among them are observation and written tests. Early on in the process, leaders should consider which competencies require observation and which can be assessed by other methods. For example, a review of inventory logs, orders, and clinical records is probably sufficient to assess a hospital pharmacist's documentation skills, but observation would be necessary to assess aseptic technique and compounding procedures.

Identifying and Providing Resources for Continuous Improvement

Leaders plan for continuous maintenance and improvement of staff members' skills. This includes orientation, individualized training, in-services, and other forms of staff development. By committing resources to learning and development activities, leaders send a message that they are committed to providing patients with the best quality of care possible by hiring highly competent staff, and that they are committed to helping staff grow and develop as individuals.

Methods for Assessing Continuing Competence

Continuing competence assessment involves the validation by a qualified person of an individual's competence in performing identified competencies on a periodic basis. Descriptions of various ongoing competence assessment methods are published in the professional literature. Dorothy J. delBueno, EdD, RN, CNAA, describes two distinct phases of evaluating a competency:[3]

- an evaluation of the individual's ability to perform the skill or achieve the desired outcome; and
- an evaluation of the individual's ability to achieve consistent performance of the skill.

She suggests that the second phase is much more difficult to define and measure.

JCAHO competency standards do not require use of any specific competence assessment method—only that the methods established by hospital leaders are followed and appropriate for the skills being assessed.

Key assessment methods include observation, written tests, and documentation. The method used often depends on the type of care and services provided, the number and type of employee or personnel under contract, and organizational resources. For example, leaders may decide that observation, written tests, and documentation are necessary to establish the following competencies for a respiratory therapist:

- Adult and/or pediatric assessment (test and documentation);
- Collection of data and interpretation of ventilator settings (documentation);
- Performance of routine and preventive maintenance of ventilators (observation);
- Performance of tracheostomy changes (observation); and
- Provision of patient education (observation).

Using Observation and Documentation Methods

One hospital that developed a clinical competency-testing program for emergency nurses identified both observation and written documentation methods as appropriate for the assessment of nurses' skills.[2] A leadership team developed a systematic approach to skill test selection. The approach involved

- listing skills regularly performed and rating them according to complexity;
- rating skills according to their frequency of occurrence; and
- considering those skills, the lack of which could cause concern in the area of patient risk (such as invasive monitoring).

The team considered the psychomotor and cognitive components of each skill or procedure. In critical care areas such as chest drainage, both observation of a sequential set of psychomotor actions and a written test to assess cognitive knowledge of proper functioning and care of chest tubes were considered appropriate. The team used a pass-fail system with the observation of psychomotor skills. The incorrect performance of steps deemed "necessary to perform" because of patient or staff concerns or mandatory standards of care resulted in automatic failure. Cognitive skills were evaluated by multiple-choice or true-false examinations.

Methods That Hospitals Can Use

Hospitals can use many methods that combine approaches based on observation and written documentation to assess staff competence in providing care that meets the special needs and behaviors of specific patient age groups. They include
- peer review of daily work performance;
- interviews using pre-established age-specific scenarios;
- observation during daily work;
- self-assessment through internally developed programs or modules developed by professional organizations;
- professional registration and certification;
- completion of selected continuing education program hours;
- patient satisfaction questionnaires and other outcome data; and
- a pay-for-performance system that gives an employee a percentage or dollar pay increase if he or she meets all required performance expectations.

Checklists, tests, skill labs, and quizzes are helpful tools in assessing competence but should not be relied upon exclusively for competence validation. Direct observation is essential for validating staff members' performance with patients. Hospitals should require supervisors to use direct observation of performance in their competence-assessment process.

Competence in serving special patient populations must be included as part of the total performance-evaluation process. Some hospitals accomplish this, in part, by requiring supervisors to complete a checklist form to evaluate an employee's competence in providing care to each patient age group.

Hospitals may wish to include on every employee's annual evaluation a provision that asks supervisors to judge whether that employee can adequately assess age-specific data and interpret age-specific responses in providing appropriate care. For employees who do not provide direct patient care, supervisors can check off "not applicable." Random chart reviews can also be used to make competence determinations on evaluations.

Interviews Using Special Patient Population Scenarios. Interviews can focus on tasks that a staff member might perform in his or her role of providing care to different patient groups. If hospital staff already have developed scenarios for teaching or competence testing, special patient population competence-validation measures can be built into these scenarios. Special patient population scenarios provide the person conducting the interview with the flexibility to modify and add to the scenario as the interview progresses. For example, a perioperative education coordinator could describe various types of patients, such as a school-age children and older adults, who are to undergo a surgical procedure and ask perioperative nurses how their care plans might vary by age of patient.[4] It is important, however, to be consistent with what is asked of each individual interviewed and how it is asked. Variability in the wording of questions may elicit different responses. Acceptable and unacceptable responses should be identified in advance.

Assessing Competence of Contract Staff

The competence of staff under contract can be assessed in a number of ways, each of which is acceptable to the Joint Commission standards, including:
- the contracting hospital's assessing the contracted employees;
- requiring contract employees to provide proof of general and special patient population competence, as applicable, as part of their contractual responsibilities;

- reviewing the contract organization's competence process to determine whether it meets the contracting hospital's specifications—if it does, appropriate documentation is provided to the hospital; and
- arranging with the outside agency's qualified individual to conduct the competence assessment of the contract staff.

Hospitals can choose to perform the competence assessment, obtain a copy of the competence assessment performed by the contract organization, or obtain a letter or memorandum of certification of completed competence assessment from the contract organization.

For personnel hired through contractual arrangements, hospitals should maintain a written job description and a completed assessment, evaluation, or appraisal tool for each individual. Evidence of these elements of successful performance must be present for each contract employee.

Observation

Observation involves a supervisor, peer, or other appropriate person monitoring an individual's performance of an activity. It may occur on the job while the individual is actually doing his or her job, or it may take place in another setting, such as a laboratory, office, or room removed from the staff member's environment of care or usual work environment. Simulated procedures may be used to demonstrate competence when an actual person for whose care the staff member is responsible is absent. For example, it is acceptable to demonstrate CPR on a mannequin. Role-playing and demonstrations of interventions or equipment are other examples. The important thing is that the individual being assessed is actually performing the activity under the observation of the person assessing him or her.

Observation may be the best and perhaps only way to validate some competencies, such as venipuncture procedures by registered nurses and

compounding procedures by pharmacists. These skills require direct observation for proper assessment. Not every competency for every position needs to be observed, however. For example, a nurse's competence in understanding the signs and symptoms of hypoglycemia could be accomplished through a written test. Hospital leaders must determine those competencies that cannot be evaluated properly except by observation, as well as how that observation will take place.

Use of Multiple Assessment Methods. Some competencies may require the use of multiple assessment methods. For example, one hospital required the use of both a written examination and observation for the assessment of pharmacists' and technicians' competencies in antineoplastic drug preparation—a high-risk process.[5] The individual's competence in chemotherapy precautions could be assessed using a written examination. Drug preparation and disposal of drug waste competencies required observation for proper assessment. Example 3-1, Competencies Assessed for Hospital Pharmacists and Technicians, page 80, illustrates the hospital's plan for competencies assessed during the first year of its comprehensive competence assessment program. The table includes reasons for selection of the competencies, staff assessed, key points assessed, and assessment methods.

A thorough tool used to assess the competence of speech and language therapists in shown in Example 3-2, Competency-based Performance Measurement Standards: Speech and Language Therapist, on pages 81-90. Each competency-based performance expectation is defined, as are the criteria for measurement based on special patient populations. Assessment methods include both review of open and closed clinical records and observations by self, peers, and supervisors. A discussion/comment sheet appears for each performance expectation, allowing both the evaluator and employee to comment on goal achievement and improvement opportunities.

It is critical that competencies being observed be documented by the person assessing the individual's competence. To this end, checklists used by the observer during the observation can facilitate such documentation. Example 3-3, Observer Checklist for Aseptic Techniques on page 91 is a sample competency validation checklist used during observation.

Written Tests and Documentation

Written tests, computer-based interactive skills exams, and other ways of assessing competence through documentation can be used for competencies that do not require observation. Written tests work well when the competency involves knowledge that can be memorized or measures that must be calculated. For example, knowledge of medication uses and contraindications might be assessed through a written exam. Other competencies that might be evaluated using written tests include identification of hazardous materials and wastes, emergency procedures, and disease-specific knowledge.

To assess pharmacists' competencies in clinical information retrieval, one hospital developed a written, 20-question, multiple-choice examination that reflected the types of drug information questions commonly encountered by pharmacists.[6] To assess age-specific competencies of perioperative staff, one hospital developed several written tools for a variety of staff members.[4] As the first part of the age-specific competence assessment process, all perioperative staff—including registered nurses, surgical technologists, operating room assistants, post-anesthesia care unit (PACU) attendants, and nursing services assistants—were required to pass a multiple-choice test on a self-study learning model covering development across the life span. The second part of the process used a written, narrative format, case scenario approach for each type of caregiver that placed patients within the context of a perioperative experience.

For example, scenarios for perioperative nurses described a six-year-old undergoing a tonsillectomy, an adolescent undergoing orthopedic surgery requiring a long rehabilitation period, and an older adult undergoing cataract surgery. Nurses being assessed were asked to develop a care plan for each patient, which was reviewed by the individual assessing their competence in age-specific perioperative care. Surgical technologists also received three case scenarios with multiple-choice questions designed to test their decision-making and critical-thinking patient care skills.

Maintaining and Improving Competence through Training and Education

A complete competence assessment program involves more than assessing competence. It also entails maintaining and improving existing skills. Therefore, hospitals should encourage self-development and continued learning for all individuals working for the hospital. High-performing hospitals create a culture that appreciates and is receptive to new ideas and knowledge by emphasizing the connection between learning and improvement. They equip staff with the tools and skills needed to translate new ideas into improvements.

Orientation, training programs, and in-service courses should address those areas identified through competence assessment that need improvement. The hospital must provide educational resources for the specific learning needs identified through the assessment process. Continuing competency-based education ensures that staff maintain proficiency in areas that are specific to their jobs, their departments, and the patient population served. Figure 3-1, on page 72, The Process of Maintaining Staff Competency, illustrates the steps involved in maintaining staff competency.

Training

Hospitals also must provide training related to any new equipment or new or revised processes used by

Figure 3-1

THE PROCESS OF MAINTAINING STAFF COMPETENCY

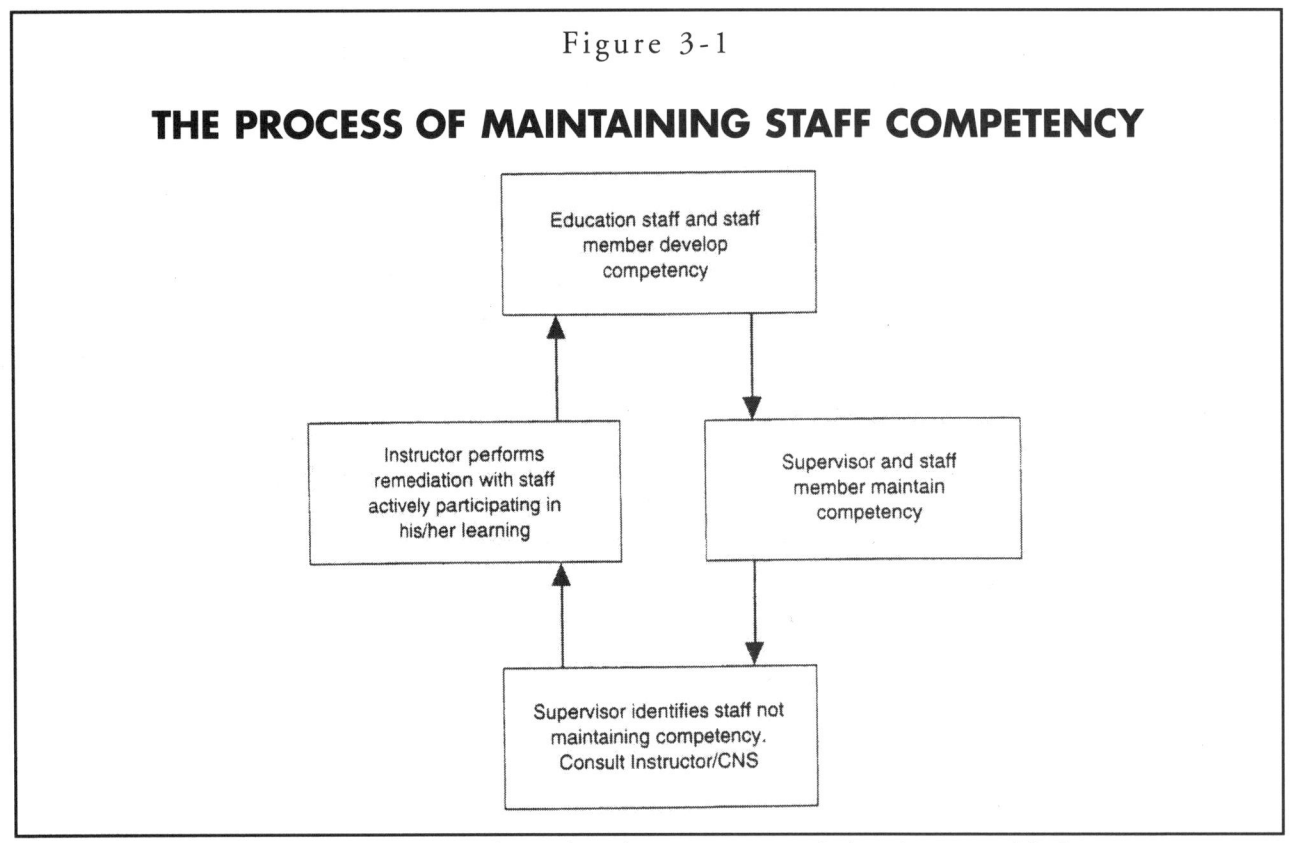

Maintaining staff competency is an ongoing process that involves education, assessment, further education, and further assessment.
SOURCE: Miller E, Flynn JM, Umadac, J: Assessing, developing, and maintaining staff's competency in times of restructuring. *J Nurs Care Qual* 12(6): 9–17, Aug 1998. Used with permission.

the individual, or any competency issues identified through a review of quality data and indicators. The Management of Human Resources standards describes how hospitals are required to periodically review each staff member's ability to carry out job responsibilities, especially when introducing new procedures, techniques, technology, and equipment.

One hospital instituted for all nurses a day-long program called "Professional Day," which gives nurses the opportunity to maintain and improve their competency in selected areas—among them are:

- hospital-required, mandatory yearly education, such as fire and safety review;
- universal precautions;
- hazard communication;
- infection control practices;
- emergency preparedness; and
- health and safety policies review.

In addition, nurses are given a chance to improve their competency to care for medical-surgical or critical care patients. The competencies offered are identified by data that indicate a need for improvement or are recommended by staff and educators. Recent offerings include competencies for managing a patient who receives epidural pain medication, blood transfusions, suctioning procedures, and tracheotomies—procedures that pose a high risk if not performed correctly. As described by two of the hospital's leaders, "Staff receive and offer a return demonstration for each technique, generally spending about 15 to 30 minutes at each station."[4]

Education

Continuing education can take a wide variety of forms, including lectures, one-on-one instruction, audiovisual programs, simulations and role-playing, self-instruction modules, and on-site training.

Creativity is often needed to design programs that are effective from both an educational and a cost perspective. Because everyone learns differently, it is helpful to identify individuals' preferred or best ways of learning during the orientation process. For example, some people retain more if they hear material rather than having it presented in written form. Others can more readily grasp a technique by performing it themselves under the guidance of an instructor, rather than watching someone else do it. Active learning almost always leads to better retention than lecturing alone. In view of this, many hospitals hold skills days or equipment days during which employees can learn new skills or how to use new technology and review existing procedures in an informal atmosphere.

In-services and Self-learning Programs

Hospitals also can educate staff about age-specific care through in-services and self-learning. Self-learning packets are frequently used to introduce staff to age-specific requirements. They contain information related to the physical, motor/sensory, cognitive, and psychosocial characteristics and needs of specific patient populations, and describe the interventions for which health care practitioners must demonstrate proficiency by age group.

To this end, some hospitals create an age-specific care and competence database and use it to periodically test staff competence. Staff members complete quizzes online and send them to the education department, where they are printed out and inserted in the employees' files. Other hospitals show relevant videos, for example, on the psychological effects of hospitalization for pediatric, adolescent, and elderly patients, after which employees are expected to take a brief self-evaluative quiz that assesses how well they understood the material.

Regular in-services (one or two a year) relating to patients who have specific conditions that are treated frequently on a patient care unit, supplement and enhance the self-learning packets. Patient care, unit-specific training material that is accompanied by a test to determine competence can be helpful. Age-specific practice guidelines developed by professional organizations also can be helpful tools, as they are designed to help practitioners choose appropriate health care interventions.

It is vital for hospitals to develop ways to encourage self-development and learning regarding age-specific patient care. Such methods include

- a self-assessment or skills checklist;
- a proficiency ladder with recognition, pay, or a bonus tied to skills enhancement;
- paid continuing education time;
- skills labs; or
- a schedule and variety of in-services based on identified needs, offered at convenient times.

A requirement of the continuing competence assessment process is that an individual's education be documented. Pages 45 and 46 of Example 2-2 are used for documenting an employee's pursuit of continuing education opportunities and attendance of in-services.

Using Data to Identify and Address Staff Improvement Needs

JCAHO standards require the collection, aggregation, and analysis of data to determine staff learning needs. Hospitals must collect and analyze aggregate data on competence patterns and trends to identify and respond to learning needs. The hospital may extract these data from performance evaluations, performance improvement efforts, risk management reports, patient satisfaction surveys, staff surveys, or other needs assessment methods.

For example, data from risk management reports may indicate an increase in needlestick injuries, signaling the need for additional training. Unusual occurrence reports may indicate a problem area. Data from patient satisfaction surveys may indicate that patients were discharged from the hospital without adequate education in wound infection prevention, signaling the need for additional training of staff responsible for wound management patient education before discharge. Performance improvement data can identify processes for which variation is almost always related to the performance of individuals. Actions to reduce variation may require clinical practice changes.

The assessment process involves gathering data. A simple competence assessment sheet used to record competence assessment findings collects data on each employee's level of proficiency in each competency. By aggregating the assessment findings for each group of employees and keeping track of trends in performance, leaders can identify more accurately the need for educational programs and resources.

Assessment data can also be trended for a specific individual to identify a baseline of competence and measure improvements. For instance, a new employee might be asked to fill out a skills checklist for self-evaluation of competencies. This self-assessment is then confirmed (or corrected) by a supervisor's assessment and used to establish learning needs and goals. Subsequent assessments, which may be recorded in matrix form throughout the employee's length of employment, track the employee's progress and can proactively identify weak areas.

Annual Reports on Competency

JCAHO requires hospitals to report at least annually to the governing body on levels of competence, patterns and trends, and competence maintenance activities. Reports to the board or other body should be concise and provide the big picture. Such a report might include
- a description of the hospital's ability to evaluate each individual's performance through a defined performance review process;

- a summary of the types of individuals evaluated, including employees, volunteers, students, contracted or agency staff, and their status;
- a summary of staff competence levels by job category;
- a description of actions taken to address staff who do not meet performance expectations, including educational efforts, and their results; and
- a prioritization and assessment of educational activities.

The report to the governing body on competence assessment and maintenance activities might be included in one annual report that covers all areas, such as safety and emergency preparedness, or it might be a stand-alone report.

What Surveyors Look For

Initial and continuing assessment of competence is covered in many activities throughout the survey, including leadership interviews, the human resources interview, review of personnel records, and on-site visits. This section covers the items surveyors look for in assessing a hospital's continuing competence assessment process.

The Leadership Interview

During the leadership interview, the surveyor asks leaders to describe the hospital's process for defining, assessing, maintaining, demonstrating, and improving the competence of all staff members on a continuing basis. For all leaders, questions specific to ongoing competence assessment might include
- How do you ensure that the competence of all staff members is assessed, maintained, demonstrated, and improved on an ongoing basis?
- How do you encourage and support staff self-development and learning?

For department or service directors, questions specific to assessing initial competence might include
- How do you determine staff's training and educational needs?

- In forensics, what education do you provide to staff who do not have clinical training or experience but who interact with patients?
- How do directors determine whether staff are competent to perform assigned duties and, when appropriate, provide care for the special needs and behaviors of specific age groups?

For nursing leaders, questions specific to assessing initial competence include

- What processes have you designed and implemented to assess, maintain, demonstrate, and improve the competence of all nursing staff members on a continuing basis?
- What aggregate data are available on a continuing basis regarding staff competency patterns and trends that may be used to identify and influence staff learning needs?

The Human Resources Interview

During the human resources interview, the surveyor also asks about the continuing competence assessment process. The emphasis here is on how the planned process is implemented on a day-to-day basis. The surveyor addresses such issues as the competence assessment process and how learning needs are identified and prioritized. Questions specific to continuing competence assessment might include

- What evidence exists of a process to ensure that each staff member participates in continuing in-service education sessions and other related training to increase his or her knowledge of specific work-related issues?
- How does the hospital determine what education and training to provide staff?
- What internal data, such as findings from infection control, safety management programs, and performance improvement activities, are used to identify staff training and education needs?
- What aggregate data are available on a continuing basis regarding staff competency patterns and trends that may be used to identify and influence staff learning needs?

- How are competency-based assessment activities documented for each staff member?
- Does the hospital consider the special needs and behaviors of specific age groups in defining the qualifications, duties, and responsibilities of staff who do not have clinical privileges but who have regular clinical contact with patients?

Review of Personnel Records and Unit Visits

During the document review session, the surveyor reviews the hospital's annual report to the governing body regarding staff competence and management minutes and reports citing the trends and patterns in staff competence that are revealed. During visits to services or units, the surveyor may talk to clinical and support/administrative staff who provide care or services regarding continuing education and training and the ways in which staff are assessed for continuing competence. Questions asked of staff might include

- How does the department manager determine whether staff are competent to perform assigned duties and, when appropriate, provide care for the special needs and behaviors of specific age groups?
- How do supervisors encourage and support staff self-development and training?
- Does each staff member participate in continuing in-service education sessions and other related training to increase his or her knowledge of specific work-related issues?

Hospitals might consider using the Competence Assessment Checklist that appears as Table 3-1 on page 76, to identify areas of the hospital's competence assessment program that may be missing. Remember that leaders will be asked about the overall process and planning, whereas staff will be asked about specifics of the program as it is used in the hospital.

Table 3-1

Competence Assessment Checklist

Process Review

- We have a process for competence assessment.
- Competencies have been identified for all staff, including full- and part-time employees, contract staff, and volunteers on all shifts.
- The frequency of assessment for each type of staff member has been established.
  — Individuals are assessed at hire.
  — Individuals are assessed at least once every three years (two, if required).
- Methods for assessing competence for each type of staff (for example, skills demonstration, records review, education, and licensure verification) have been defined.
- The qualifications of persons performing assessments for each type of staff member have been defined.
- Results of assessments are aggregated and used to plan continuing staff education.
- Individuals take part in appropriate education and training to maintain and improve competence.

Personnel Record Review (sample at least one record for each type/level of staff)

- Competencies/required skills have been defined for this individual.
  — Competencies for special patient populations are documented if required.
- Competence assessments have been conducted at the intervals specified by the hospital.
- Competence assessments have been performed by a qualified individual.
- Competence assessments have included the methods defined by hospital leaders as necessary for this staff member (for example, skills demonstration, records review, education, and licensure verification).
- This staff member has received continuing education and training pertinent to his or her competence/skill requirements.

SOURCE: Brushing up on competence assessment. *Joint Commission Perspectives* 21(1):6–7, Jan 2001.

Common Problems in Assessing Continuing Competence

Results from recent surveys indicate that nearly one-third of all hospitals had trouble complying with the standard related to assessment of each staff member's ability to meet the performance expectations stated in his or her job description. Among the trouble spots for many accredited hospitals in the area of assessing continuing competence are timeliness of assessments; assessing age-specific competence; lack of parallelism between job descriptions and performance evaluations; problems with the aggregation and analysis of data, and assessing, maintaining, demonstrating, and continually improving the competence of all staff members.

Timeliness of Assessments

For many hospitals, timeliness of assessments is the major source of difficulty related to this standard. Hospital leaders must define the frequency required for performance assessments and ensure that they are performed within the prescribed time frame. If a hospital's policy requires annual assessments, then hospital staff must be able to provide data indicating the percentage of assessments that were completed on time.

Improvement Tips. The following tips can minimize the chances of the organization failing to meet JCAHO standards of compliance in the area of ongoing competence assessment:

- Ensure that all staff—including part-time employees—receive performance evaluations that assess ongoing competency, and ensure timely evaluations according to hospital policy. If the policy isn't realistic, revise it. Staff include not only full-time staff but also volunteers and contract staff. Understand that the competence assessment requirements relate to more than just the nursing staff. Dietary, laundry, maintenance, and housekeeping staff are among the staff included in this requirement.
- Set up tickler files for performance evaluation dates.

Competencies for Special Patient Populations

For many hospitals, another major challenge with regard to this standard is assessing the competencies of staff in relating to special patient populations, particularly those who have clinical contact. The knowledge and skills required of each position must be tailored to job classifications and the age-related needs of patients served. Passing a test on growth and development is not enough. Staff members must demonstrate competence in dealing with special patient populations; evidence of this must be provided to the surveyor. More than "head knowledge" is required; application of that knowledge to the job at hand is also a must.

Improvement Tip. Use forms or tools to ensure that competencies involving special patient populations are part of an employee's regular performance evaluation and that they can be documented efficiently.

Lack of Parallelism Between Job Descriptions and Performance Evaluations

Another common compliance problem is the failure of performance evaluations to reflect an individual's job description. The tool used to evaluate a staff member's performance should be tailored to the job. All-in-one job description/performance evaluation tools can work well for organizations. Employees quickly see the expectations and how they will be measured. By contrast, with generic evaluation tools, the employee never gets true feedback for actual performance.

Documentation of the competence assessment process can be problematic for some hospitals. Common problems include lack of documentation on competence assessment tools, incomplete or missing orientation checklists, inconsistent competence assessment documentation from department to department, inadequate documentation of staff participating in continuing education programs, and lack of documented competencies for per diem, pool, agency, and contract personnel.

Improvement Tips. The following three tips can minimize the problems created by the failure of performance evaluations to reflect an employee's job description:

- Use job descriptions to create tailored performance evaluation tools.
- Consider developing a combined job description or performance evaluation tool. List job responsibilities on the left and the scoring method on the right.
- Understand that there are no short cuts for complying with this standard. It is hard work, but can be made easier with a well-defined process.

Problems with the Aggregation and Analysis of Data

The aggregation of competence data and identification of staff learning needs have been problematic for some hospitals, as well. Hospitals must have processes for identifying staff learning needs and for meeting them. Collected, aggregated, and analyzed data provide the starting point for achieving this.

Improvement Tip. Compliance problems in this area can be overcome by improving the process by which data are collected.

- Hospitals can collect data pertaining to learning needs through staff surveys, performance evaluations, performance improvement activity reports, or other needs assessments.
- If the majority of employees perform poorly on a particular post-program test item after participating in an in-service session, the need for learning opportunities can be identified and addressed.

Continually Improving the Competence of All Staff Members

Finally, hospitals often may have difficulty meeting the JCAHO Management of Human Resources standard of assessing, maintaining, demonstrating, and continually improving the competence of all staff members. Indeed, hospitals that have trouble complying with earlier standards typically do not perform well with this standard either.

When new procedures, techniques, or equipment are introduced, staff competence must be evaluated. If a hospital's staff cares for specialty patient populations, such as postpartum, infants, or children—even if care is delivered on a limited basis to a limited number of patients—staff competence in each specialty area should be assessed. Observation is an essential part of the assessment process. Although written tests and self-assessments can be part of the process, they cannot be the only methods used. Demonstration of staff competence requires observation of the skills being assessed.

Improvement Tips. To reduce the difficulties in this area of compliance with competency standards, hospitals should

- determine the frequency with which each performance expectation must be assessed. (If an activity is performed by the person many times each day, it may not need to be evaluated or assessed as often after an initial assessment.)
- ensure that assessments are performed according to established frequencies.
- define, incorporate, and assess special patient population competence for all staff who have direct patient contact. A matrix that displays each performance competency, the associated skills, knowledge, attitudes, and frequency of evaluation, is a tool that works well for some hospitals.

Reports to the Governing Board on Continuing Competence Assessment

Reports to the governing board on levels of competence, patterns and trends, and staff education activities, must occur as described in the standards and their intents. They should be comprehensive, indicate performance by job categories, identify areas that require improvement, and indicate the remedial steps that are being taken in the areas found wanting. Although the Joint Commission does not specify a reporting format, surveyors note that high-quality reports usually are set up in matrix format, with job categories listed in the left-hand column and performance ratings (such as unsatisfactory, average, above average, and so forth) across the top of the page, and totaled to show aggregate scores.

Improvement Tips. The following strategies can help hospitals improve their chances of securing a favorable rating from the Joint Commission in the area of reporting to the hospital's governing board:

- Develop a plan that identifies the data that will be collected and how the plan will be accomplished.
- Collect data for all staff, including contract staff.

- Be selective about the data that are to be collected and analyzed. Hospitals should pick one or two studies and make sure leaders and staff understand them well. It is critical that they select staff competence studies based on what is important to the hospital and where the greatest risks lie.

- Include a brief narrative describing areas that need improvement and steps taken to address those areas in the hospital's report to the governing body on competence.

REFERENCES

1. Britton BP, Raper JT, Walden CM: From development to evaluation: Making a competency plan work. *J Nurs Staff Dev* 11(4): 210–214, Jul/Aug 1995.

2. Ready RW: Clinical competency testing for emergency nurses. *J Emerg Nurs* 20(1): 24–32, Feb 1994.

3. delBueno DJ: Competence, criteria, and credentialing. *J Nurs Admin* 23:7–8, May 1993. Cited in Parsons EC, Capka MB: Building a successful risk-based competency assessment model. *AORN J* 66(6): 1065–1071, Dec 1997.

4. Chard RR: Using a case scenario approach to evaluate age-specific competencies. *AORN Journ* 67(3): 634–642, Mar 1998.

5. Marshall JM, Adams JP, Janich JA: Practical, ongoing competency-assessment program for pharmacists and technicians. *Am J Health-Syst Pharm* 54:1412–1417, Jun 15, 1997.

6. Martin AE, Stumpf JL, and Ryan ML: Assessing pharmacists' competence in clinical information retrieval. *Am J Health-Syst Pharm* 53:2957–2958, Dec 15, 1996.

Example 3-1

Competencies Assessed for Hospital Pharmacists and Technicians

Competency	Reason for Selection	Staff Assessed	Key Points Assessed	Assessment Method
Point-of-care distribution system[a]	High-volume, problem-prone	All pharmacy staff with access to system	Refilling medications, removing medications, preparing reports	Demonstration to validator
Aseptic technique	High-risk, high-volume	Pharmacists and technicians working in i.v. preparation area	Knowledge of requirements for aseptic preparation, scrub procedure, hood cleaning, sterile technique	Multiple-choice examination, observation by validator, commercially available test kits
Antineoplastic drug preparation	High-risk	Pharmacists and technicians working in oncology satellite pharmacy	Chemotherapy precautions, drug preparation, disposal of drug waste	Multiple-choice examination, observation by validator
TPN[b] preparation	High-risk, problem-prone	Pharmacists in i.v. preparation area	Assessing orders for drug compatibility and stability, calibration of automated compounder,[c] use of refractometer	Open-book examination, demonstration to validator
Neonatal TPN preparation	High-risk, problem-prone	Pharmacists in neonatal intensive care unit	Products used in neonatal TPN preparation, dosage calculations, compatibility and stability	Open-book examination
Calculations	High-risk, problem-prone	All technicians	Basic mathematics for ordering and stock control, metric-system measures and conversions, calculations for preparation of i.v. products	Closed-book examination
Solid-dose prepackaging	High-volume	All technicians	Operation of prepackaging system,[d] record keeping	Closed-book examination, including example entries in a simulated unit dose log
Assessment of drug therapy	High-volume, high-risk, problem-prone	All pharmacists	Dosage adjustment in renal impairment, vancomycin and ciprofloxacin drug-use evaluations, pharmacokinetics of digoxin, theophylline, and phenytoin	Closed-book examination
Medical emergencies	High-risk	All pharmacists	Indications, dosage, and preparation of drugs used in medical emergencies	Open-book examination

[a]Pyxis MedStation. Pyxis Corporation. San Diego, CA.
[b]TPN = total parenteral nutrition
[c]Automix compounder. Clintec Nutrition Company. Deerfield, IL.
[d]Baxter ATC212 system. Baxter Healthcare Corporation. Deerfield, IL.

SOURCE: Marshall JM, Adams JP, Janich JA: Practical, ongoing competency-assessment program for pharmacists and technicians. Originally published in *American Journal of Health-System Pharmacy* 54:1412–1417, Jun 15, 1997. All Rights reserved. Reprinted with permission.

Example 3-2

Competency-based Performance Measurement Standards for Speech and Language Therapist

RATING SCALE

GENERAL

0. Generally fails to meet performance expectations
1. Sometimes does not meet performance expectations
2. Meets performance expectations consistently
3. Meets and frequently exceeds the standards
4. Significantly exceeds performance expectations on most occasions

PERCENTAGES

0. Meets performance expectation 79% or less of the time
1. Meets performance expectation 80% - 84% of the time
2. Meets performance expectations 85% - 89% of the time
3. Meets performance expectations 90% - 94% of the time
4. Meets performance expectations 95% - 100% of the time

EXCEPTIONS

0. There are 7 or more documented exceptions to standard per year
1. There are 5-6 documented exceptions to standard per year
2. There are 3-4 documented exceptions to standard per year
3. There are 1-2 documented exceptions to standard per year
4. There are zero documented exceptions to standard per year

Note:
For any rating of "0" or "1", the employee is not meeting expected level of performance and an action plan must be developed to address performance and/or educational needs. The action plan will be documented and performance will be monitored during the period of the corrective action plan.

PROVISION OF POSITION SPECIFIC SERVICES

COMPETENCY BASED PERFORMANCE EXPECTATION	CRITERIA FOR MEASUREMENT	RATING BASED ON	INITIAL REVIEW	1ST ANNUAL	2ND ANNUAL	3RD ANNUAL	4TH ANNUAL	5TH ANNUAL
Evaluation and treatment planning: Selects and performs the appropriate assessment procedures based on accepted practice standards and according to approved hospital policies and procedures.	**ALL AGES:** Based on a review of 10 or more open and closed charts per year and on observations by self, peers and supervisors, the employee demonstrates the following have been assessed: history, mental status, pain, communication status, speech, language, oral and pharyngeal sensorimotor function.	___ GENERAL ___ PERCENT ___ EXCEPTIONS						
	NEONATES Based on a review of 10 or more open and closed charts per year and on observations by self, peers and supervisors, the employee demonstrates the following additional areas have been assessed: APGAR scores, gestational age, oral motor skills, parental involvement and educational needs.	___ GENERAL ___ PERCENT ___ EXCEPTIONS						
	PEDIATRICS Based on a review of 10 or more open and closed charts per year and on observations by self, peers and supervisors, the employee demonstrates the following additional areas have been assessed: parental involvement in educational needs; availability of support personnel within the school system; and family involvement in follow-up at home.	___ GENERAL ___ PERCENT ___ EXCEPTIONS						
	ADOLESCENTS: (12 years to 18 years) Based on a review of 10 or more open and closed charts per year and on observations by self, peers and supervisors, the employee demonstrates the following additional areas have been assessed: related peer involvement/support or social issues, parental involvement and special interests/hobbies that might promote successful outcomes.	___ GENERAL ___ PERCENT ___ EXCEPTIONS						
	GERIATRICS Based on a review of 10 or more open and closed charts per year and on observations by self, peers and supervisors, the employee demonstrates the following additional areas have been assessed: consideration of the affects of aging on function	___ GENERAL ___ PERCENT ___ EXCEPTIONS						

HRJ/JOBDESC/JDST01
© 2001 Angela M. Phillips, Images. All Rights Reserved. From: The Desktop Consultant – The Rehab Department's Guide to JCAHO

(continued on next page)

EXAMPLES

Competency-based Performance Measurement Standards for Speech and Language Therapist (continued)

EXAMPLES

Page 2

COMPETENCY BASED PERFORMANCE MEASUREMENT STANDARDS: SPEECH AND LANGUAGE THERAPIST

COMPETENCY BASED PERFORMANCE EXPECTATION	CRITERIA FOR MEASUREMENT	RATING BASED ON	INITIAL REVIEW	1ST ANNUAL	2ND ANNUAL	3RD ANNUAL	4TH ANNUAL	5TH ANNUAL
Establishes and updates a formal plan of care to address individualized patient needs during hospitalization and upon discharge.								
Initiates a written plan of care within 48 hours of referral to include physical, psychosocial, environmental, and educational and discharge needs as related to therapy.	**ALL AGE GROUPS** Based on a review of 10 or more open and closed charts per year and on observations by self, peers and supervisors, the employee demonstrates the following areas have been assessed: documentation includes key factors (deficits noted, priority of treatment, plan of care, goals in functional terms, times for goal achievement, prognosis, barriers, facilitators, contraindications/ precautions, home environment, educational needs, psychosocial areas and discharge planning).	___ GENERAL ___ PERCENT ___ EXCEPTIONS						
	NEONATE Based on a review of 10 or more open and closed charts per year and on observations by self, peers and supervisors, the employee demonstrates the following additional areas have been assessed: parent/caregiver involvement in determining the neonate's readiness for treatment, and tolerance to intervention.	___ GENERAL ___ PERCENT ___ EXCEPTIONS						
	PEDIATRIC Based on a review of 10 or more open and closed charts per year and on observations by self, peers and supervisors, the employee demonstrates the following additional areas have been assessed: parent involvement in the plan of care, and play activities as part of treatment.	___ GENERAL ___ PERCENT ___ EXCEPTIONS						
	ADOLESCENT Based on a review of 10 or more open and closed charts per year and on observations by self, peers and supervisors, the employee demonstrates the following additional areas have been assessed: parent involvement in the plan of care, peer activities, and special interests are considered.	___ GENERAL ___ PERCENT ___ EXCEPTIONS						
	GERIATRICS Based on a review of 10 or more open and closed charts per year and on observations by self, peers and supervisors, the employee demonstrates the following additional areas have been assessed: treatment plan reflects modified exercises to address changes due to the effects of aging.	___ GENERAL ___ PERCENT ___ EXCEPTIONS						

(continued on next page)

Competency-based Performance Measurement Standards for Speech and Language Therapist (continued)

COMPETENCY BASED PERFORMANCE MEASUREMENT STANDARDS: SPEECH AND LANGUAGE THERAPIST

Page 3

COMPETENCY BASED PERFORMANCE EXPECTATION	CRITERIA FOR MEASUREMENT	RATING BASED ON	INITIAL REVIEW	1ST ANNUAL	2ND ANNUAL	3RD ANNUAL	4TH ANNUAL	5TH ANNUAL
Assesses effectiveness of treatment plan.								
Documents patient response to treatment and progress toward goals.	**ALL AGE GROUPS** Based on a review of 10 or more open and closed charts per year and on observations by self, peers and supervisors, the employee demonstrates competence in the following areas: treatment notes reflect actual treatment and response; progress toward goals is addressed at least on a weekly basis; and progress is measured related to functional abilities; treatment time is recorded on every visit.	___ GENERAL ___ PERCENT ___ EXCEPTIONS						
	ALL AGE GROUPS Based on a review of 10 or more open and closed charts per year and on observations by self, peers and supervisors, the employee demonstrates competence in the following areas: when patient fails to make progress toward goals, documentation addresses reasons and care is modified; when patient is progressing as expected, reevaluation occurs every 2 weeks; members of the care team and the patient and family are involved in treatment planning	___ GENERAL ___ PERCENT ___ EXCEPTIONS						
	ALL AGE GROUPS Based on a review of 10 or more open and closed charts per year and on observations by self, peers and supervisors, the employee demonstrates competence in the following areas: When a change in care plan occurs based on physician orders, a reassessment is done prior to initiation of the new treatment.	___ GENERAL ___ PERCENT ___ EXCEPTIONS						
	ALL AGE GROUPS Based on a review of 10 or more open and closed charts per year and on observations by self, peers and supervisors, the employee demonstrates competence in the following areas: IP: reassessments are completed at least every 2 weeks. OP: reassessments are completed at least every 30 days.	___ GENERAL ___ PERCENT ___ EXCEPTIONS						
	ADOLESCENT Based on a review of 10 or more open and closed charts per year and on observations by self, peers and supervisors, the employee demonstrates competence in the following additional areas: when the adolescent fails to make progress as expected; peer or sibling involvement is considered in modification of the plan of care.	___ GENERAL ___ PERCENT ___ EXCEPTIONS						
	NEONATE/PEDIATRIC Based on a review of 10 or more open and closed charts per year and on observations by self, peers and supervisors, the employee demonstrates competence in the following additional areas: when the neonate or pediatric patient fails to make progress as expected; the participation of the parent or caregiver is considered in modification of the plan of care.	___ GENERAL ___ PERCENT ___ EXCEPTIONS						

(continued on next page)

Competency-based Performance Measurement Standards for Speech and Language Therapist (continued)

EXAMPLES

Page 4

COMPETENCY BASED PERFORMANCE MEASUREMENT STANDARDS: SPEECH AND LANGUAGE THERAPIST

COMPETENCY BASED PERFORMANCE EXPECTATION	CRITERIA FOR MEASUREMENT	RATING BASED ON	INITIAL REVIEW	1ST ANNUAL	2ND ANNUAL	3RD ANNUAL	4TH ANNUAL	5TH ANNUAL
Supervision of the ancillary staff.								
Delegates appropriate therapy activities to ancillary therapy staff members; and directs and supervises staff members consistent with state laws and in a safe and effective manner.	Based on observation by self, peers and/or supervisors and on survey data collect orally or in written form from ancillary staff members supervised, meets this performance expectation.	___ GENERAL ___ PERCENT ___ EXCEPTIONS						
Develops and revises interventions and programs as needed to achieve positive patient outcomes and to meet the needs of the patient population served.	Based on observation by self, peers and/or supervisors and on survey data collect orally or in written form from ancillary staff members supervised, meets this performance expectation.	___ GENERAL ___ PERCENT ___ EXCEPTIONS						
Provision of speech and language therapy care.								
Utilizes treatment modalities in accordance with accepted standards of care and in accordance with departmental policies and procedures	**ALL AGE GROUPS** Based on a review of 10 or more open and closed charts per year and on observations by self, peers and supervisors, the employee demonstrates competence in the following areas: therapeutic program or activities provided; frequency and duration; and response to treatment when not as expected.	___ GENERAL ___ PERCENT ___ EXCEPTIONS						
	ALL AGE GROUPS Based on a review of 10 or more open and closed charts per year and on observations by self, peers and supervisors, the employee demonstrates competence in the following areas; treatment is provided in a manner that is safe and within acceptable practice; treatment is provided in a safe and comfortable environment and distractions are minimized unless being incorporated into the treatment program.	___ GENERAL ___ PERCENT ___ EXCEPTIONS						
	ALL AGE GROUPS Based on test for knowledge based competencies, is able to pass proficiency testing at appropriate accuracy levels.	___ GENERAL ___ PERCENT ___ EXCEPTIONS						
	PEDIATRICS Based on a review of 10 or more open and closed charts per year and on observations by self, peers and supervisors, the employee demonstrates competence in the following additional areas: the caregiver recognizes the importance of involvement of the parent, caregiver, peer or sibling in the treatment process.	___ GENERAL ___ PERCENT ___ EXCEPTIONS						
	GERIATRICS Based on a review of 10 or more open and closed charts per year and on observations by self, peers and supervisors, the employee demonstrates competence in the following areas: caregiver recognizes when it is or is not appropriate to use amplification devices.	___ GENERAL ___ PERCENT ___ EXCEPTIONS						

(continued on next page)

Competency-based Performance Measurement Standards for Speech and Language Therapist (continued)

Page 5

COMPETENCY BASED PERFORMANCE MEASUREMENT STANDARDS: SPEECH AND LANGUAGE THERAPIST

COMPETENCY BASED PERFORMANCE EXPECTATION	CRITERIA FOR MEASUREMENT	RATING BASED ON	INITIAL REVIEW	1ST ANNUAL	2ND ANNUAL	3RD ANNUAL	4TH ANNUAL	5TH ANNUAL
Performs swallow studies in accordance with accepted standards of care and in accordance with departmental policies and procedures.	**ALL AGE GROUPS** Based on a review of 10 or more open and closed charts per year and on observations by self, peers and supervisors, the employee demonstrates competence in the following additional areas: clearly describes treatment, instructs patient in safety issues; and assures patient is in safe and comfortable position for evaluation and treatment. **ALL AGE GROUPS** Based on observations by self, peers and supervisors, the employee demonstrates competence in the following additional areas: follows universal precautions when appropriate and assures safety during treatment by communicating to support staff needs and positioning requirements. **PEDIATRIC** Based on a review of 10 or more open and closed charts per year and on observations by self, peers and supervisors, the employee demonstrates competence in the following additional areas: the caregiver recognizes that the pediatric client has special safety needs and will be fearful of treatment and encourages parent or caregiver to be involved in treatment as appropriate. **GERIATRIC** Based on a review of 10 or more open and closed charts per year and on observations by self, peers and supervisors, the employee demonstrates competence in the following additional areas: caregiver recognizes that the geriatric client has special safety needs, assures that the dignity of the patient is protected during feeding programs and provides additional time for treatment as appropriate.	___ GENERAL ___ PERCENT ___ EXCEPTIONS						
Provides effective instruction to the patient and family through standardized educational programs and individualized training	**ADOLESCENTS, ADULTS, GERIATRICS** Based on periodic observation by self, supervisor, peers: education is given using language and demonstration appropriate to the level of the patient and the care giver confirms understanding by return demonstration, vocalization of the information or other acceptable manner. **GERIATRICS** Based on periodic observation and on review of documentation: provides written materials in large print when needed. **PEDIATRICS/NEONATES** Based on periodic observation by self, supervisor, or peers: education is given using language and demonstrations appropriate to the level of the patient. When a parent or caregiver is present, that individual is included in the educational process.	___ GENERAL ___ PERCENT ___ EXCEPTIONS						

HR/JOBDESC/JDST01

(continued on next page)

Competency-based Performance Measurement Standards for Speech and Language Therapist (continued)

COMPETENCY BASED PERFORMANCE MEASUREMENT STANDARDS: SPEECH AND LANGUAGE THERAPIST

Page 6

COMPETENCY BASED PERFORMANCE EXPECTATION	CRITERIA FOR MEASUREMENT	RATING BASED ON	INITIAL REVIEW	1ST ANNUAL	2ND ANNUAL	3RD ANNUAL	4TH ANNUAL	5TH ANNUAL
Documents the education given, to whom it was given and level of comprehension of the information or demonstration	**ALL AGE GROUPS** Based on a review of 10 or more open and closed charts per year, documentation demonstrates that the following were completed and documented in accordance with the department standards: When education program is given, documentation includes a statement of who was educated, a copy of the instructions is included in the chart or a clear description of the program documented the day it was given, and a statement assessing patient/family understanding or demonstration of independence with the exercise	___ GENERAL ___ PERCENT ___ EXCEPTIONS						
Discharge Planning. Based on initial assessment findings and early response to treatment plans for post- discharge needs of the patient (equipment, further care, home program)	**ALL AGE GROUPS** Based on a review of 10 or more open and closed charts per year and on observations by self, peers and supervisors, the employee demonstrates competence in the following areas: equipment needs were identified, home program was established, when extended care or home care was needed, recommendations were made.	___ GENERAL ___ PERCENT ___ EXCEPTIONS						
	ALL AGE GROUPS Based on a review of 10 or more open and closed charts per year and on observations by self, peers and supervisors, the employee demonstrates competence in the following areas: the family was involved in discharge plans when appropriate.	___ GENERAL ___ PERCENT ___ EXCEPTIONS						
	NEONATE/PEDIATRIC Based on a review of 10 or more open and closed charts per year and on observations by self, peers and supervisors, the employee demonstrates competence in the following areas: as part of discharge planning, the parent or alternative caregiver is educated in any home care or exercise required	___ GENERAL ___ PERCENT ___ EXCEPTIONS						
Communicates with patient, family, care givers, significant others and members of the healthcare team to promote maximum benefit of care.								
Identifies patient/family ability to communicate with the provider verbally and nonverbally	**ALL AGE GROUPS** Based on a review of 10 or more open and closed charts per year and on observations by self, peers and supervisors, the employee demonstrates competence in the following areas: primary language indicated, communication status documented	___ GENERAL ___ PERCENT ___ EXCEPTIONS						
Seeks alternate forms of communication when necessary (interpreters, communication boards)	**ALL AGE GROUPS** Based on a review of 10 or more open and closed charts per year and on observations by self, peers and supervisors, the employee demonstrates competence in the following areas: when primary language is not English, an interpreter or alternate communication tools were used and when verbal communication was not possible, alternative forms of communication were used	___ GENERAL ___ PERCENT ___ EXCEPTIONS						

HR/JOBDESC/JDST01
© 2001 Angela M. Phillips, Images. All Rights Reserved. From: The Desktop Consultant – The Rehab Department's Guide to JCAHO

EXAMPLES

(continued on next page)

Competency-based Performance Measurement Standards for Speech and Language Therapist (continued)

EXAMPLES

COMPETENCY BASED PERFORMANCE MEASUREMENT STANDARDS: SPEECH AND LANGUAGE THERAPIST

Page 7

SAFETY: Provides an environment that is conducive to the safety of patients visitors and staff by maintaining knowledge of safety, assessing the risks for safety; implementing precautions when a risk is identified and complying with hospital and departmental policies on fire, safety, evacuation plan, disaster plan , MSDS, infection control, universal precautions and OSHA guidelines.

COMPETENCY BASED PERFORMANCE EXPECTATION	CRITERIA FOR MEASUREMENT	RATING BASED ON	INITIAL REVIEW	1ST ANNUAL	2ND ANNUAL	3RD ANNUAL	4TH ANNUAL	5TH ANNUAL
Identifies needs/problems related to real or potential safety risks to patients, visitors, employees and self based on interpretation of available information and implements interventions as related to identified real or potential safety risks	ALL AGE GROUPS Based on documented exceptions to desired standards: Incidents, complaints or observations of failure to meet the standard will be documented by the supervisor and placed in the employee's file.	___ GENERAL ___ PERCENT ___ EXCEPTIONS						
Demonstrates safe body mechanics during patient care and support activities.	ALL AGE GROUPS Based on periodic observation of treatment by self, peers and/or supervisors, the following conditions are met: bends at hips and knees using a straight back bend, uses assistance when necessary, avoids reaching or bending over fulcrum.	___ GENERAL ___ PERCENT ___ EXCEPTIONS						
Follows standard precautions when appropriate.	ALL AGE GROUPS Based on periodic observation of treatment by self, peers and/or supervisors, the following conditions are met: wears appropriate protective gear, follows clean to dirty protocol, uses good hand washing techniques, disposes of sharps according to hospital policy	___ GENERAL ___ PERCENT ___ EXCEPTIONS						
Supports safety monitoring and reporting for the department	Based on periodic observations by self, peers or supervisors and on documented exceptions noted, demonstrates competence in this area.	___ GENERAL ___ PERCENT ___ EXCEPTIONS						
Complies with policies and procedures that guide and support a safe environment	Based on periodic observations by self, peers or supervisors and on documented exceptions noted, demonstrates competence in this area.	___ GENERAL ___ PERCENT ___ EXCEPTIONS						
Complies with policies and procedures that guide and support the appropriate application of restraints	ALL AGE GROUPS Based on periodic observation of treatment by self, peers and/or supervisors, the following conditions are met: applies restraints using correct procedures; notifies nursing staff when issues arise related to the use of restraints; participates in identification of alternatives to the application of restraints; documents application of restraints consist with policy	___ GENERAL ___ PERCENT ___ EXCEPTIONS						

HRJJOBDESC/JDST01

(continued on next page)

Competency-based Performance Measurement Standards for Speech and Language Therapist (continued)

COMPETENCY BASED PERFORMANCE MEASUREMENT STANDARDS: SPEECH AND LANGUAGE THERAPIST

Page 8

COMPETENCY BASED PERFORMANCE EXPECTATION	CRITERIA FOR MEASUREMENT	RATING BASED ON	INITIAL REVIEW	1ST ANNUAL	2ND ANNUAL	3RD ANNUAL	4TH ANNUAL	5TH ANNUAL
PROFESSIONALISM AND CUSTOMER SERVICE								
Communicates necessary information to team members, listens objectively, portrays a positive image and attitude and addresses concerns through established processes at the appropriate time.	Based on periodic observations by self, peers or supervisors and on documented exceptions noted, demonstrates competence in this area.	___ GENERAL ___ PERCENT ___ EXCEPTIONS						
Maintains appropriate licensure and certifications required for position and attends all mandatory education within 30 days of date due	Based on periodic observations by self, peers or supervisors and on documented exceptions noted, demonstrates competence in this area.	___ GENERAL ___ PERCENT ___ EXCEPTIONS						
Consistently follows all hospital policies and procedures	Based on periodic observations by self, peers or supervisors and on documented exceptions noted, demonstrates competence in this area.	___ GENERAL ___ PERCENT ___ EXCEPTIONS						
Attendance meets acceptable standards.	Based on periodic observations by self, peers or supervisors and on documented exceptions noted, demonstrates competence in this area.	___ GENERAL ___ PERCENT ___ EXCEPTIONS						
Appearance meets acceptable standards for neatness, cleanliness, grooming and suitability of attire and is in compliance with dress code of hospital and department.	Based on periodic observations by self, peers or supervisors and on documented exceptions noted, demonstrates competence in this area.	___ GENERAL ___ PERCENT ___ EXCEPTIONS						
LEADERSHIP								
Supports the philosophy, mission, vision and values of the organization through attitude, work ethic, and behavior.	Based on periodic observations by self, peers or supervisors and on documented exceptions noted, demonstrates competence in this area.	___ GENERAL ___ PERCENT ___ EXCEPTIONS						
Identifies problems, assesses options, considers alternatives and makes recommendations for preferred solutions.	Based on periodic observations by self, peers or supervisors and on documented exceptions noted, demonstrates competence in this area.	___ GENERAL ___ PERCENT ___ EXCEPTIONS						
Participates in hospital-sponsored activities, committees, meetings and special projects.	Based on periodic observations by self, peers or supervisors and on documented exceptions noted, demonstrates competence in this area.	___ GENERAL ___ PERCENT ___ EXCEPTIONS						

HRJOBDESC/JDST01
© 2001 Angela M. Phillips, Images. All Rights Reserved. From: The Desktop Consultant – The Rehab Department's Guide to JCAHO

(continued on next page)

EXAMPLES

Competency-based Performance Measurement Standards for Speech and Language Therapist (continued)

COMPETENCY BASED PERFORMANCE MEASUREMENT STANDARDS: SPEECH AND LANGUAGE THERAPIST

Page 9

COMPETENCY BASED PERFORMANCE EXPECTATION	CRITERIA FOR MEASUREMENT	RATING BASED ON	INITIAL REVIEW	1ST ANNUAL	2ND ANNUAL	3RD ANNUAL	4TH ANNUAL	5TH ANNUAL
APPROPRIATE AND EFFECTIVE USE OF RESOURCES								
Meets department standards for productivity	Based on periodic observations by self, peers or supervisors and on documented exceptions noted, demonstrates competence in this area.	___ GENERAL ___ PERCENT ___ EXCEPTIONS						
Accounts for resources in accordance with hospital policies and procedures	Based on periodic observations by self, peers or supervisors and on documented exceptions noted, demonstrates competence in this area.	___ GENERAL ___ PERCENT ___ EXCEPTIONS						
Completes assigned tasks within time frames allocated or communicates inability to do so to supervisor	Based on periodic observations by self, peers or supervisors and on documented exceptions noted, demonstrates competence in this area.	___ GENERAL ___ PERCENT ___ EXCEPTIONS						
Accepts and completes additional assignments as appropriate	Based on periodic observations by self, peers or supervisors and on documented exceptions noted, demonstrates competence in this area.	___ GENERAL ___ PERCENT ___ EXCEPTIONS						

TOTAL POINTS THIS REVIEW:
TOTAL POINTS AVAILABLE:
%-AGE SCORE (TOTAL POINTS ACHIEVED/TOTAL POINTS AVAILABLE)
%-AGE OF SALARY INCREASE (SEE HR POLICY)

HR/JOBDESC/JDST01
© 2001 Angela M. Phillips, Images. All Rights Reserved. From: The Desktop Consultant – The Rehab Department's Guide to JCAHO

(continued on next page)

EXAMPLES

Competency-based Performance Measurement Standards for Speech and Language Therapist (continued)

PAGE 10

COMPETENCY BASED PERFORMANCE MEASUREMENT STANDARDS: ANNUAL SUMMARY

INITIAL REVIEW:

STRENGTHS	CHALLENGES	GOALS ACCOMPLISHED THIS PERIOD	GOALS ESTABLISHED FOR NEXT PERIOD	EDUCATIONAL NEEDS IDENTIFIED	HOSPITALWIDE IMPROVE-MENT OPPORTUNITIES IDENTIFIED BY EMPLOYEE

DISCUSSION/COMMENTS

EVALUATOR COMMENTS:

SIGNATURE _____ DATE

EMPLOYEE COMMENTS:

SIGNATURE _____ DATE

The performance review information above has been reviewed with me and,

☐ I agree with the information presented

☐ I disagree with the information presented because:

_____

_____

_____

_____

EMPLOYEE _____ DATE

SUPERVISOR _____ DATE

DIRECTOR _____ DATE

HUMAN RESOURCES _____ DATE

HR/JOBDESC/JDST01

Example 3-3

Observer Checklist for Aseptic Techniques

Date _____   Employee name _____
(deadline for completion of assessment:)

	satisfactory? Y	N
No jewelry or clothing to elbows. No chipping nail polish. Long hair is pulled back.		
Prepares laminar flow hood for use: Cleans top, bar, sides, back grille, and bottom with 70% isopropyl alcohol. Cleans from top to bottom, back to front.		
Scrubs hands, nails, wrists, forearms for at least 30 seconds with a brush, warm water, and appropriate bactericidal soap. Scrubs again if compromised by answering phone, retrieving dropped items from floor, touching face or hair, etc.		
Positions objects within the hood such that nothing interrupts the flow of air between the HEPA filter and sterile objects.		
Conducts all aseptic manipulations at least six inches within the hood to prevent backwash.		
Places only those items essential to product preparation in the laminar airflow hood. Nonessential materials are discarded. Other items (e.g., calculator, wax pencils, labels), if absolutely necessary, are placed no more than six inches into the hood.		
Swabs all rubber closures of vials and ampul necks with 70% isopropyl alcohol prior to aseptic manipulation.		
Inserts the proper amount of air into vials prior to withdrawal of the drug.		
Opens ampuls with a firm, snapping motion away from the HEPA filter.		
Uses filter needles correctly when withdrawing medications from ampuls.		
Manipulates syringes properly, not touching the tip or plunger. Needle caps are not laid on the hood surface if the syringe or needle will be reused.		
Injects medications through the proper port or stopper of the IV solution container.		
Does not touch or otherwise contaminate any component which should remain sterile during preparation of the admixture.		
After preparation, inspects admixture for cores or other particulate matter.		

Notes:

Verified by:

Maintaining staff competency is an ongoing process that involves education, assessment, further education, and further assessment.

SOURCE: Miller E, Flynn JM, Umadac J: Assessing, developing, and maintaining staff's competency in times of restructuring. *J Nurs Care Qual* 12(6): 9–17, Aug 1998. Used with permission.

Initial Competence Assessment of Licensed Independent Practitioners

This chapter addresses the initial stages of competence assessment for licensed independent practitioners (LIPs) covered by the Medical Staff standards. These individuals include fully licensed physicians and other licensed individuals permitted by law and by the hospital to provide patient care services independently for the hospital. It covers the means by which medical staff leadership assesses the competence of an LIP—from application for clinical privileges and appointment to the medical staff for the provision of patient care services through the granting of initial appointments and privileges.

Competence assessment for LIPs is accomplished through the credential review and privileging processes, which entail the following steps:

- Medical staff department directors recommend a sufficient number of qualified and competent persons to provide patient care or service, based on the responsibilities of the role.
- Medical staff leaders delineate the criteria for granting clinical privileges relevant to the care provided by the department, an activity comparable to that performed by department leaders for those staff covered by the Management of Human Resources standards.
- Medical staff department directors outline the performance expectations and competencies required for specific positions within the hospital.

- LIPs who wish to provide care or services for the hospital apply for an initial medical staff appointment and/or clinical privileges, providing information related to current competence, licensure, training, and experience.
- Medical staff leaders verify the information about the applicant's current ability to perform up to defined expectations and the requested clinical privileges.
- Medical staff leaders make the decision to grant or deny initial medical staff appointment and/or clinical privileges, delineating the privileges granted and spelling out any limitations or conditions.

A detailed description of each activity performed by the medical staff follows the description of JCAHO requirements.

JCAHO Requirements

A department leader is responsible for the consistent, continuing, and effective functioning of the department and for the continuous improvement of its performance. These responsibilities encompass not only the department's functioning, but also its integration into the overall functioning of the larger organization. As a result, the availability of competent and qualified persons to provide the care or service necessary to meet patients' needs is critical. So is the careful definition of the criteria used to determine whether an applicant is qualified and competent to provide that care and service.

Medical staff department directors delineate the relevant criteria for clinical privileges that pertain to the care provided by the department. These are, in effect, the competencies required of the LIPs who provide the care or services. Current competence is one of four core criteria essential to establishing and maintaining a qualified and competent medical staff. Current licensure, relevant training or experience, and ability to perform the privileges requested comprise the remaining core criteria. A hospital must verify information in each of these areas from primary sources, whenever possible, and the applicant must agree to the inspection of records and documents pertinent to his or her current competence, training, and experience. Specifically, medical staff department directors are charged with:

- establishing the criteria for clinical privileges that are relevant to the care delivered by the department;
- recommending a sufficient number of qualified and competent staff to deliver care;
- providing orientation and continuing education for all staff who work in the department or provide service;
- recommending professional criteria for clinical privileges;
- seeing to it that the professional criteria for clinical privileges pertain to evidence of current licensure, relevant training or experience, current competence, and ability to perform the privileges requested;
- verifying information about an applicant's licensure, specific training, experience, and current competence with information from the primary source whenever possible;
- basing the applicant's appointment or reappointment to the medical staff and the initial granting and renewal or revision of clinical privileges on information regarding his or her competence;

- obtaining the applicant's consent to inspect the records and documents pertinent to his or her licensure, specific training, experience, current competence, and ability to perform the privileges requested, and, if necessary, inviting the applicant in for an interview; and
- delineating an individual's clinical privileges, including limitations, if any, on his or her privileges to admit and treat patients or direct the course of treatment for the indications for which the patients were admitted.

A number of these responsibilities apply to both the initial and continuing competence assessment process, and will be discussed both in this chapter and in Chapter 5.

Defining Scope of Privileges

The scope of privileges granted by a hospital must be well defined and address the specific care or services to be provided. The competence of LIPs to perform the privileges granted as defined by the hospital should be assessed initially and on a continuing basis. Thus, assessment of competence and privileges are integrally connected. In fact, the two-part purpose of delineating privileges is to

- define the scope of a practitioner's authorized clinical activities within the organization; and
- provide a basis for assessing the practitioner's competence.

Many factors enter into a hospital's decision-making process concerning the breadth of clinical care to be provided within the facility. Care should be taken to ensure flexibility in the privileging process so as to reflect the rapid pace of change in the practice of medicine. The following factors should be considered as hospital leaders establish the scope of clinical care:

- The mission, vision, values, size, and resources of the organization determine the extent of the services it offers.
- The degree to which these medical services will be provided depends on the proportion of gen-

eralists, specialists, and sub-specialists on staff and their experience and training.

- The needs of the community served are also considered in determining the mission of an organization, the services to be provided, and the range of privileges granted to the clinical staff.

It is reasonable to expect that the scope of privileges will vary widely among health care organizations. The privileging system of a small community hospital serving a largely rural area, for example, will address a less complex scope of privileges than that of a large teaching hospital that offers a full range of tertiary services. It is important that an individual's privileges be organization specific because organization, or site-specific, privileges ensure that practitioners who provide care at multiple sites within a system or multi-state organization are practicing within the scope of care offered by each site.

To expedite the process of developing or revising a privileging system, a medical staff will occasionally adopt a privileging system from another facility without detailed review of its content. This practice may lead to inclusion of the authority to perform clinical procedures or treat disease categories that are outdated or not within the adopting hospital's mission or ability to provide. Hospitals must develop a privileging system that is tailored to individual hospital factors, such as mission, vision, resources, and patients served.

The characteristics of an organization, such as size, location, and ownership, also determine the services it provides. For instance, a hospital owned by a religious order may adhere to an additional authority. Because Roman Catholic hospitals must adhere to the ethical and religious directives of Catholic health care facilities, certain procedures generally would not be permitted, regardless of the training and experience of clinical staff. A privilege list that included the excepted procedures, therefore, would not be hospital specific.

With the proliferation of available technology, diagnostic and therapeutic options are changing rapidly. These new developments often render some clinical approaches outdated while making new ones available. The hospital's medical staff should periodically review the entire range of privileges authorized and practiced within a facility to ensure that the determination actually reflects the practice within the hospital and its appropriateness to the needs of the community it serves.

Privilege Classification Systems

Many methods of grouping or classifying privileges and procedures are used within health care organizations. Among the more common are

- lists of procedures or treatments by body part or anatomical region, or by bundles or clusters;
- patient risk categories;
- level of training and experience needed;
- required practitioner specialty;
- core privileges; and
- any combination of the methods listed above—particularly a combination of patient risk categories or core privileges and lists of procedures.

Although a thorough description of these methods is beyond this book's scope, a brief description and examples follow.

Lists of Procedures or Treatments. The "laundry list" method is probably the most common approach to privileging—especially for delineating interventional procedures. This mechanism is often found in surgical specialties such as general surgery, ophthalmology, orthopedics, gynecology, urology, and so on, but may also include specialties such as interventional radiology or interventional cardiology. This method of classification also lends itself to treatment of diseases by specialties such as family practice, internal medicine, and pediatrics.

In the laundry-list system, the medical staff provides a list of procedures or disease categories for the applicant to request. For example, delineation of privileges for emergency medicine might include airway techniques, anesthesia, cardiac procedures, diagnostic procedures, genitourinary techniques, hemodynamic techniques, orthopedic techniques, thoracic procedures, and specific privileges within each major category. Privileges within the thoracic procedures category, for example, might include needle thoracostomy, tube thoracostomy, emergency thoracotomy, and pericardiocentesis.

More complex examples of the laundry-list approach might be systems using the American Medical Association's CPT-4 coding list. Medical record personnel and practitioners' offices use the system for coding inpatient and outpatient procedures and for billing purposes. Example 4-1, Request for Clinical Privileges—Orthopedic Surgery, on pages 109–111, provides a list of orthopedic privileges as delineated by one health care organization.

Bundles or Clusters. Bundling or clustering is similar to grouping by body parts, anatomical regions, or subspecialty areas. Many of the systems using the procedure-specific (CPT-4) or disease-specific (ICD-9-CM) laundry lists are evolving into a clustering of like procedures or diseases. The clusters or bundles approach has wide appeal because it minimizes the danger that a procedure will be omitted from the listing, thereby minimizing medical-legal risk. The CPT-4 system also abbreviates the listing, thus limiting the time necessary to complete and delineate multiple requests. Example 4-2, on pages 112–115, shows the list of privileges delineated by bundles or clusters for DeKalb Memorial Hospital, Auburn, Indiana.

Patient Risk Categories/Level of Training and Experience. Classification by patient risk is more commonly used with diagnostic and treatment of disease categories or body systems and is more often found in the predominately noninvasive specialties such as internal medicine, pediatrics, and family practice. In this system, the organization

establishes categories or levels of practice—usually by complexity of disease and risk to the patient. This structure generally combines a level of training and experience with the complexity of disease and patient risk. For example, the American Academy of Pediatrics (AAP) has established progressive categories that define the extent of independent decision making and care allowed to a practitioner. These categories have been adapted from a form used by the Alfred I. duPont Hospital for Children, Wilmington, DE, to delineate pediatric privileges:

- Category I: Treatment of illness, injuries, or conditions or the performance of procedures that carry low risk for the patient. Criteria for requesting privileges include training and experience with these conditions. Eligibility includes physicians and nonphysicians.
- Category II: Treatment of major or complicated illnesses, injuries, or conditions in children with no significant risk to life. Criteria for requesting privileges include significant training in pediatrics. (Board certification in pediatrics is not necessary.)
- Category III: Treatment of major and/or complicated illnesses or performance of procedures that carry a significant threat to life. Criteria for requesting privileges include extensive training or documented experience in the care of these conditions and board certification/eligibility with active (defined in departmental rules and regulations) pursuit of certification in pediatrics a key benchmark.
- Category IV: Treatment of unusually complex or critical illnesses, injuries, or conditions or the provision of procedures for those that carry a serious threat to life. Criteria for requesting privileges include extensive post-residency or subspecialty training, or experience beyond board certification in pediatrics a key benchmark.

The AAP also has a similar classification for the treatment of newborns. The AAP links patient risk categories with criteria for granting the privilege.

Criterion-based privileging is discussed later in this chapter.

During the process of determining whether this classification system is applicable to a specific hospital, the medical staff should evaluate the appropriateness of the categories for the pediatric patient population served. In a small hospital, for example, perhaps only the first three categories would apply. Conceivably, only visiting consultants would be allowed category IV privileges—if the hospital provides those services.

Core Privileges. Although not specifically mentioned in the Joint Commission standards, the core classification concept has recently received attention for the same reasons that the bundling or clustering method has. The theory behind this method is that a "core" of knowledge and skill is included within a given area of training. Therefore, upon completion of specified training (for example, an obstetrics/gynecology residency), a practitioner should be competent to treat a core group of diseases and conditions or perform certain categories of procedures. Any disease or procedure beyond the core would then require evidence of additional training or experience and necessitate a separate privilege request.

The benefit of core privileging is that it reduces the need for separate evaluation of training, experience, current competence, and outcome for privileges that are similar in the knowledge or skills required. This method simplifies the processing of privilege applications and the monitoring of privilege use. Example 4-3, General Surgery—Core Privileges, on pages 116–118, is the form that the Department of the Navy uses to identify core and supplemental privileges.

Combination of Systems. Because the various specialties of clinical practice are complex, it is often not possible to select a single system of classification for procedures and diseases. Many organizations, there-

fore, use a combination of systems. Combinations occur most often in specialties in which cognitive and procedural privileges are merged. Examples would be psychiatry, internal medicine, and pediatrics. In these specialties, the practitioner diagnoses and treats by body system/specialty area but also may perform a limited number of interventional procedures such as arterial puncture, bladder tap, lumbar puncture, and thoracentesis.

There may be no single perfect approach for classifying procedures, diseases, or conditions for the purposes of granting specific privileges. What is right for one hospital or department may not be right or appropriate for another. The organization will sometimes have three or more approaches or combinations evident. Some methods lend themselves to surgical specialties, whereas others are more appropriate for noninvasive diagnostic and therapeutic specialties. Therefore, privileging should match not only the hospital's needs but also the needs of individual departments, sections, or specialties. See Sidebar 4-1, Guidelines for Defining Categories of Privileges, below.

Sidebar 4-1

Guidelines for Defining Categories of Privileges

- Consider how the categories will be used to assess practitioner competence.
- Ensure that all of the procedures or clinical conditions within a category require the same cognitive and technical skills.
- Ensure that privileges are practitioner-specific. There must be a mechanism to add procedures or to delete them from the predetermined categories.

Criterion-Based Privilege Delineation

Whatever system is used for classifying procedures to grant specific privileges as described above, privileging must be criterion-based. Pre-established criteria ensure that the medical staff applies the same decision-making processes to each applicant. The Joint Commission requires that each clinical department make recommendations to the medical staff regarding professional criteria for clinical privileges. These criteria are then specified in the medical staff bylaws (or policies and procedures, or rules and regulations) and are uniformly applied to all applicants for delineated clinical privileges. These criteria

- constitute the basis for granting initial, renewed, or revised clinical privileges;
- are designed to assure the medical staff and governing body that patients will receive quality care; and
- pertain at least to evidence of current licensure, relevant training or experience, current competence, and ability to perform the privileges requested.

Criterion-based privileging establishes "a level playing field" for the applicant and provides the basis for recommending privileges on objective evidence of current competence. Using pre-established criteria minimizes the impact of favoritism or friendship on the decision-making process and reduces opportunities for charges of prejudicial treatment from the applicant or re-applicant. Thus, if an initial applicant does not meet the privileging criteria, the request for privileges does not receive consideration.

When the medical staff uses a system involving classification or categorization of privileges, the scope of each level of privileges must be well defined, and the requirements to be met by the applicant are stated clearly for each category. Example 4-4, the University Hospitals of Cleveland's Department of Family Medicine Requirements for Specialized Procedures, on pages 119–121, illustrates an outline of the requirements for specialized procedures performed by family practitioners.

Competence and the Application Process

With a clear definition of the scope of privileges that can be granted in the hospital, the organization is ready to receive applications for medical staff membership and/or clinical privileges. The medical staff and governing body determine which LIPs may apply for medical staff membership and clinical privileges and which may apply for clinical privileges without membership. The medical staff bylaws should clearly state which LIPs are allowed to request medical staff membership and which are allowed to request only delineated clinical privileges. Figure 4-1, an application flow diagram for applying for privileges, page 99, illustrates the application process from start to completion.

The Credentialing Process

An individual's application to the organization for medical staff membership and/or clinical privileges begins the credentialing process. The purpose of credentialing is to ensure that LIPs are qualified to provide care and can do so within the limits of their competence and also within the capacity of the organization to support those activities. Applications typically contain information regarding personal and demographic information, education and training, licensure, board certification, hospital affiliations, and other details. Also included in applications typically are professional references from peers who have current knowledge of the applicant's competence.

Competence and the Verification Process

Upon receipt of a completed application for initial appointment or clinical privileging, a practitioner's current competence must be verified and evaluated by the appropriate medical staff body. Organizations are required to perform primary source verification whenever feasible relative to licensure, training and

Figure 4-1

APPLICATION FLOW DIAGRAM

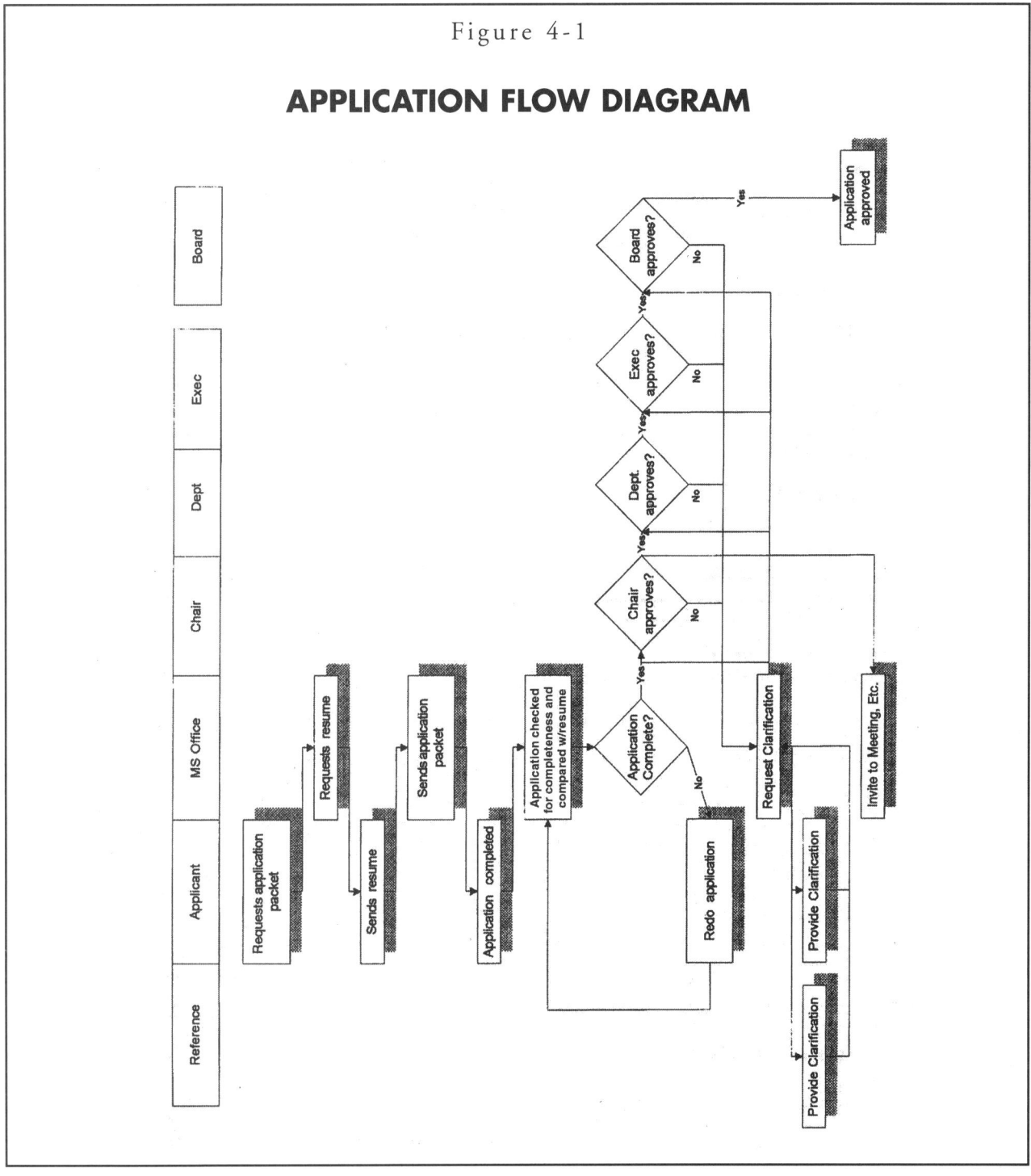

SOURCE: Carson Tahoe Hospital, Carson City, NV. Used with permission.

experience, current competence, and ability to perform the privileges requested. Primary source verification requires information directly from the originating source. Copies of diplomas, certificates, and licenses do not constitute primary source verification. Additionally, documents that are hand delivered or provided directly from the practitioner are not primary source verification. Primary source verification for licensure, specific training, experience, and current competence can be performed using various methods and resources.

Verifying current competence during the credentials review and privileging process involves determining an individual's current capability to perform up to defined expectations. Graduation from professional schools, specialty training, or board certification, does not tell the whole story. Instead, letters from individuals who are personally knowledgeable about the applicant's professional and clinical performance in teaching facilities or other health care organizations provide the necessary verification.

To verify current competence, information is obtained from peers who are personally knowledgeable about the applicant's current professional and clinical performance. Peer recommendations can confirm that the applicant is in good health; that he or she is able to perform the requested privileges; and address the applicant's training, experience, current competence, and past fulfillment of obligations. Example 4-5 on page 122 is a cover letter sent by one hospital to peers identified by the applicant for medical staff appointment and privileges. The letter requests information related to the applicant's

- current clinical competence;
- performance of clinical judgment and technical skills;
- ethical character;
- physical and emotional health status; and
- ability to work cooperatively with others.

Asking for such information in narrative form rather than as check-offs on a questionnaire encourages the peer to elaborate fully, using more open-ended responses.

Obtaining Information on Competence

One of the most efficient ways to obtain information on competence is to send a questionnaire to current department chairs, chiefs of staff, or peers as described earlier. The questionnaire should contain questions regarding the scope and level of the applicant's abilities and performance. Questions must be included regarding the applicant's fulfillment of obligations as a member of the medical staff at all hospitals with which the applicant was or is currently affiliated.

If an LIP does not have a hospital practice, as might occur with family practitioners who refer to hospitalists, for example, a credentials committee can evaluate his or her current clinical competence by obtaining letters of recommendation from individuals who receive referrals from the practitioner and other physicians in the community.

Writing to Peers. For applicants who have completed training and have practiced for several years, writing to a peer at the institution where the applicant has a practice will provide information on experience and current competence. Information is usually obtained from the chair of the department, although other appropriate sources of information may be the vice president of medical affairs and the chair of the performance-improvement committee. In any case, information on current competence must be obtained from a peer, preferably an MD or DO from the same medical specialty as the applicant. A podiatrist's peer (DPM) is another podiatrist (DPM). Doctors of dental surgery (DDSs) and doctors in dental medicine (DDMs) also are peers. Peer recommendations are required in credentials review. These references can be obtained from training institutions, hospitals where the applicant is currently practicing, and other professional references provided by the applicant.

Most dentists, oral surgeons, podiatrists, psychologists, certified registered nurse anesthetists, and so on have professional contact with others in their peer group, regardless of whether they practice in the same hospital. These resources should be tapped if there is no peer within the health care organization. On occasion, a community is so small that there are no other practitioners in the individual's peer group within the community. In such instances the local professional society can be contacted to determine whether information can be obtained from a dental or podiatric association. In the case of renewal of privileges, a peer from outside the community might be asked to review a selection of patient records or directly observe surgical procedures and provide comment.

For high-risk procedures, it is useful to request information on the applicant's current competence specific to that privilege. For instance, if the applicant is requesting privileges to perform cardiac catheterization, information regarding the number of procedures performed and the mortality and morbidity rates should be requested from the medical director of the catheterization laboratory where the applicant is currently practicing.

Additional Evidence of Competence. When an LIP has extensive clinical privileges granted from another hospital, but does not provide such services there, it often is difficult for the hospital to verify his or her competence with the requested privileges. In such cases, the hospital can inform the applicant that it cannot verify competence in the requested clinical privileges unless the applicant provides evidence of performing the privileges at another health care organization and/or provides evidence of continuing education related to the privileges.

Organizations that grant privileges must evaluate the practitioner's ability to perform the privileges requested; this evaluation must be documented in the individual's credentials file. The applicant's statement that there is no condition that would affect his or her ability to perform the privileges requested is often obtained on the application form. This statement must then be confirmed. Confirmation for applicants from training can be obtained from residency or fellowship directors on the same form used to confirm the completion of training. In the case of physicians who are twenty or more years beyond training, the level of detail required by the training reference questions will not be obtainable.

For an applicant who has been in practice for some years, confirmation can be obtained from department chairpersons where the applicant currently holds privileges or by another peer who is currently knowledgeable about the applicant. Example 4-6, page 123, a credentialing worksheet from UHHS Bedford Medical Center in Ohio, can be used to track progress throughout the verification process.

Making the Decision to Appoint and/or Grant Privileges

After all verifications have been received and any "red flags" have been investigated and resolved, the hospital's department chair or authorized individual reviews the information, interviews the applicant (if required), and makes a recommendation on the appointment and privileges. The granting of clinical privileges to a practitioner to provide specific care and services in an organization within well-defined limits can be made only by the appropriate authority based on the practitioner's qualifications and demonstrated competency. Action on an application for appointment and privileges must be withheld until verification is complete. The decision-making process must

- take into consideration quality-of-care criteria;
- be non-discriminatory;
- occur within a specified time frame; and
- be the same process for medical staff members, non-medical staff members, employed or contract LIPs, and administrative physicians.

The recommendation for appointment and clinical privileges is forwarded to the credentials committee, if applicable, where all information is available for review (if required). The recommendations of the department chair (or, in instances in which a hospital does not have departments, the chief of staff) and credentials committee (if applicable) are forwarded to the medical executive committee, who makes further comments and recommendations. The recommendations of the department chair, credentials committee (if applicable), and medical executive committee are forwarded to the governing board for final resolution regarding appointment and privileges. Example 4-7 on pages 124–125 is a sample department chair initial appointment assessment/recommendation form.

The governing board has the option of delegating the decision. If the governing board is responsible for appointing practitioners and granting privileges, a letter of appointment is sent to the practitioner. It should include the date of appointment and its expiration, the department to which the practitioner has been appointed (if applicable), the staff category and status, a copy of the clinical privileges granted, and any other information deemed appropriate.

If the governing board denies or limits appointment or clinical privileges, the medical staff's fair hearing and appeal process may be instituted, if allowed. In many cases, the fair hearing and appeal process is initiated if and when the medical executive committee makes an adverse recommendation. The hearing and appeal process must be documented in the medical staff and governing body bylaws.

Delineating Clinical Privileges

All individuals who are permitted by law and the hospital to provide patient care services independently in the hospital must have delineated clinical privileges regardless of whether they are medical staff members. This requirement refers to individuals who may not be allowed staff membership by law, as well as individuals who are permitted by law to be members of the medical staff but not by the hospital. For example, some states require that clinical psychologists be members of the medical staff if they are to be granted clinical privileges. In most

hospitals, however, psychologists generally are not members of the medical staff. Nevertheless, in either case, if psychologists are permitted to provide patient care services without clinical supervision or direction, the hospital and its medical staff must grant them clinical privileges to provide the service.

The delineation of an individual's clinical privileges must include the limitations, if any, on the individual's privileges to admit and treat patients or direct the course of treatment for the conditions for which the patients were admitted. Thus, if a limited-license practitioner (for example, psychologist, certified nurse midwife, nurse practitioner) is allowed admitting privileges, the privileging list must clearly state that fact. Likewise, if a practitioner is not allowed independent admitting privileges, the privilege delineation system should also specify that limitation. For most medical staff members, the right to admit patients can be covered in a simple statement in the bylaws or rules and regulations and need not be repeated in each individual's delineated privileges. The credentialing and privileging process is assumed to ensure age-specific competencies for LIPs. Privilege delineations often specifically address special needs and behaviors of specific patient age groups treated by the LIP.

Proctoring

Despite the use of rigorous credentials review and evaluation processes by medical staff services professionals, medical staff department chairs and credentials committees, instances occur in which practitioners request and are granted privileges for which there is no assurance of their competence. Reasons for this include
- inadequate evidence of current competence;
- lack of knowledge on the part of the individual providing an evaluation/recommendation of the applicant's actual performance, or hesitation to assess the practitioner honestly or objectively;
- hesitancy on the part of those responsible for limiting the privileges requested; and

- differences in available equipment or support personnel in the new setting.

Proctoring of newly privileged individuals is one measure that can be used to attempt to ensure that the credentials review and evaluation process was accurate relative to the privileges granted. Proctoring is a process by which an individual is reviewed and evaluated to ensure competence. It is used most frequently for high-risk privileges or during an observation period at an LIP's initial appointment. A proctor is the person who performs the assessment. Proctoring can also help to ensure that LIPs new to practice in the hospital are clinically competent before they receive clinical privileges to perform requested procedures.

In medical staff organizations, the term *proctor* means to observe, supervise, mentor, oversee, or directly assess. Proctoring may take on many meanings and may be defined differently by each organization, depending on the circumstances. Methods include direct observation, concurrent and retrospective review of clinical records, and an assessment of the LIP's interpersonal skills vis-à-vis other LIPs, nurses, and ancillary personnel.

Reasons for Proctoring

Most commonly, proctoring is conducted because of a need for
- a systematic approach to evaluating and monitoring newly privileged practitioners;
- a method to evaluate and monitor individuals who have requested an additional privilege;
- a means for an individual to develop and demonstrate additional skills or knowledge in a particular area of practice; and
- a mechanism to assess a practitioner whose competence is in question.

In delineating an individual's clinical privileges, proctoring may be a condition specified for a certain period of time for identified privileges before the individual's independent performance of

them. In effect, the proctoring period functions as an orientation period after which the LIP should be fully competent to perform the privilege on his or her own. The hospital should consider how (and when) expectations during the proctoring period and progress toward meeting the goals will be communicated to the individual.

Although proctoring of invasive procedures is much easier to conceptualize and accomplish, the process also lends itself to noninvasive specialties such as medicine, pediatrics, and psychiatry. It enables established medical staff members or other individuals who have privileges to help new individuals assimilate into the organization's environment. Proctoring also helps the organization's employees to feel confident of the new practitioner's skills because of the tacit assurance from the proctor.

JCAHO's Position on Proctoring

The Joint Commission does not specifically require proctoring; nor does it define the process when it occurs in an organization. It does, however, encourage each organization to individually determine, based on its needs, what mechanism would best meet the standards and their intent statements. As organizations consider whether to institute a proctoring process, many factors must be considered. Among them are the reasons for proctoring, the process that may apply to each circumstance, and the desired outcome.

Policies on Proctoring

Policies on proctoring may range from the very simple to the complex. For example, at one hospital:
- The first 15 major elective surgical procedures must be observed by a member of the surgery or obstetrics and gynecology department (whichever is applicable). A total of 70% of the cases observed must be by a member of the individual's subspecialty, if applicable. If the individual is in a partnership or group practice, no more than 20% of the cases should be

observed by a surgeon in the partnership or group.

- If the individual is unable to arrange for an observer, he or she should contact the chairman of the applicable department or an alternate who will either assign an observer or waive the requirement. Emergency procedures, when feasible, should also be observed. These requirements should be completed within a period of six months but that period may be extended. If any of the observed cases are believed to be unsatisfactory, the observation requirement may be extended for a maximum of two years.

The Proctor/Practitioner Relationship

Obviously, continuing dialogue between the proctor and the practitioner is paramount to the success of any proctoring process. If individuals being proctored are open to discussing their diagnostic and/or therapeutic choices, the goals of the monitoring process are more readily achieved. The ability and tact of the proctor in offering constructive comments, and the willingness of the practitioner to incorporate these suggestions into future practice patterns are at the heart of a successful proctoring process.

Similarly, the willingness of the proctor to learn new approaches or techniques contributes to his or her knowledge base. Realistically, in a non-teaching hospital, many practitioners are infrequently exposed to the newest or latest techniques and instrumentation or diagnostic and therapeutic modalities, except through articles or lectures. Many educators argue that participation in a process provides a more effective method of learning. Thus, proctoring also provides an opportunity to continuously maintain or improve the performance of practitioners who serve as proctors.

Proctoring as a Method of Assessment

The outcome of the proctoring process should not only serve as a method of evaluating newly privi-

leged individuals or individuals who request an expansion of privileges, but should also be a continuous source of information against which the credentials verification and evaluation and privileging process can be measured. If the proctoring process demonstrates that a practitioner is not sufficiently competent to maintain a granted privilege, the individuals involved in the credentials review/privileging process should evaluate the process retrospectively.

The lessons learned might lead to establishment of additional privileging criteria or to an increase in the level of the existing criteria. Perhaps the credentials verification process should be enhanced to obtain more comprehensive clinical information. Lack of surprises or negative outcomes in the proctoring process is one indicator that the initial credentials review, evaluation, and privileging mechanisms are excellent.

At times the proctoring process can be used (even if proctoring is not the routine) to grant a privilege for which there is some reservation. The privileging process may have identified a specific procedure or disease entity for which questions about the applicant's qualifications exist. Proctoring thus can be used to evaluate the individual's competence to perform the specific procedure or manage the specific disease entity. Example 4-8 on page 126 illustrates the proctoring form that one hospital uses to evaluate an individual's competence in performing surgical procedures.

Granting Temporary Privileges

Privileges granted on a temporary basis might be appropriate if they are granted judiciously under very specific circumstances. The following two circumstances exist for which the granting of temporary privileges is acceptable:

- To fulfill an important patient care need; and
- When an applicant with a complete, clean application is awaiting review and approval

from the medical staff executive committee and the governing body.

In the first circumstance, temporary privileges can be granted on a case-by-case basis when an important patient care need mandates an immediate authorization to practice, for a limited period of time, while the full credentials information is verified and approved. Examples would include, but are not limited to,

- a situation in which a physician becomes ill or takes a leave of absence and an LIP would need to cover the practice until the physician returns; and

- an instance in which a specific LIP has the necessary skills to provide care or perform a procedure that no LIP currently privileged possesses and that is needed in the care of a particular patient.

Under these circumstances, the CEO or his or her designee may grant temporary privileges upon the recommendation of either the applicable clinical department chairperson or the president of the medical staff, provided current licensure and current competence has been verified.

In the second circumstance, temporary privileges may be granted when the new applicant for medical staff membership or privileges is waiting for the medical staff executive committee's review and recommendation and the governing body's approval. Upon the recommendation of either the applicable clinical department chairperson or the president of the medical staff, the CEO may grant temporary privileges for a limited period of time, provided that

- the applicant's current licensure has been verified;

- the applicant possesses the relevant training or experience;

- the applicant demonstrates current competence;

- the applicant is able to perform the privileges requested; and

- other criteria required by medical staff bylaws have been met.

In addition, the results of a National Practitioner Data Bank (NPDB) query must have been obtained and evaluated, and the applicant must have a complete application, with no current or previously successful challenge to licensure or registration, has not been subject to involuntary termination of medical staff membership at another organization, and has not been subject to involuntary limitation, reduction, denial, or loss of clinical privileges.

Temporary privileges are not to be routinely used for other administrative purposes, such as when an LIP fails to provide all information necessary to the processing of his or her reappointment in a timely manner, or the failure of the staff to promptly verify performance data and information.

Duration of Temporary Privileges

Temporary privileges are granted only for a limited period of time, determined by the medical staff and defined in the medical staff bylaws. The duration often is granted for a period of 30 or 60 days and can be renewed for an additional 30 days. The most important factor when considering granting temporary privileges is patient care. Such privileges should not be used for strictly administrative reasons, but they can be considered in the event of a patient care or medical need. When weighing the granting of temporary privileges, the medical staff and hospital must evaluate the associated risks of granting privileges to a practitioner about whom full information has not been obtained. Additionally, the hospital's need to provide appropriate and timely medical care to members of the community must also be considered.

Locum Tenens

Locum tenens means "to hold a place." In the health care world, a locum tenens is a person, such as a physician, who substitutes temporarily for another. The number of locum tenens physicians who work only in part-time, temporary assignments has grown significantly in past decades. In 1987, for instance, 4 percent of physicians practiced on a locum tenens basis; by 2000, this figure had increased to 15 percent.[1] The desire for time off to travel, to navigate through a life transition such as a divorce, to care for a family, and the wish for increased mobility and freedom from administrative paperwork are reasons cited for such growth. Physicians older than age 50 comprise most locum tenens physicians, but those younger than age of 35 are the fastest growing group.[2] Approximately one-third of locum tenens physicians come from residency programs.[2]

Occasions may arise when the only physician in a specialty (for example, pathology, radiology) is ill, and a locum tenens physician is recruited to provide the necessary patient care services for a specified time period until the medical staff member can resume his or her practice. Temporary privileges often are granted in such a situation. Nevertheless, from a medical and legal perspective, every effort must be made to document and assess current competence.

It is often difficult to evaluate competency when practitioners work for very short periods of time and move frequently. Locum tenens physicians who have worked for short durations of time at many institutions and whose experience and references are verified only by the contracting entity that serves as the employment agency pose a high risk. Although not always feasible, it is a good practice to verify the competence and experience of locum tenens practitioners directly with the institutions where the practitioner actually worked rather than relying on second-hand reports from the contracting entity. One danger is that the LIP may have created the letters of reference attesting to competence for the locum tenens agency and that the agency did not verify these materials. The risks associated with locum tenens privileges can be higher than with other types of temporary privileges.

What Surveyors Look For

The Joint Commission evaluates the hospital's competence assessment process through review of policies, procedures, and plans that are verified through interviews, observation, and review of documents and records. Initial and continuing competence assessment is covered in many activities throughout the survey, including medical staff leadership interviews, review of credentials and privileging records, and on-site visits. Chapter 4 covers only those items that surveyors look for in assessing a hospital's initial competence assessment process for LIPs covered by the Medical Staff standards. Additional items that surveyors look for in assessing this process for LIPs are covered in Chapter 5.

During the medical staff credentials interview with the director of the medical staff and medical staff credentials committee representatives, the surveyor reviews credentials files of selected members of the medical staff and other individuals whose patient care activities are defined through the medical staff privileging process. Potential questions related to initial competence assessment include

- Do all members of the medical staff have delineated clinical privileges?
- How would you describe the process, including the criteria for appointing/reappointing and granting/renewing/revising clinical privileges?
- How do you ensure that all individuals with clinical privileges provide services within the scope of those privileges?
- How would you assess the individual's professional performance, judgment, and clinical or technical skills?

During the medical staff leadership interview, the physician surveyor meets with the president of the medical staff, medical director, medical staff coordinator, chairs or section chiefs of medical staff departments, elected and appointed leaders of medical staff, and others. A possible question related to competence assessment is: How do you use assessment findings related to an individual's performance in the peer review process, or in the continuing evaluation of LIPs' competence?

Common Problems in Assessing Initial Competence for Licensed Independent Practitioners

Several areas in assessing initial competence for LIPs present compliance problems for organizations. Among them are

- lack of uniformity of credentialing criteria;
- provision of privileges for services that the hospital does not provide and that are not defined in the scope of services;
- a credentialing process that fails to cover all practitioners; and
- insufficient evidence of an LIP's current competence.

Improvement Tip for Ensuring Uniformity

Credentialing criteria should be uniformly applied to all LIPs that apply to provide patient care services for the hospital. The most effective way to ensure the uniform application of criteria is to establish, implement, and monitor an effective credentials review and privileging process. Sometimes organizations think that they can apply the whole credentialing process to a group of individuals as one (for example, a consulting anesthesiology group that may be working for the surgery department). This is not acceptable. The process must ensure that every LIP meets the defined core criteria.

Improvement Tip for Non-provided or Undefined Services

Clinical privileges must be granted based on the practitioner's qualifications and the care provided by the organization. Privileges granted at a nearby hospital cannot be transferred wholesale to another facility. The granted privileges must be within the organization's scope of service and be site-specific. For example, hospital privileges for a surgeon to perform heart-lung transplantation cannot be granted in a hospital that does not have the capa-

bilities, support staff, and equipment to support such a service.

Improvement Tip for Failure to Cover All LIPs

All practitioners permitted by law and the organization to practice independently must be covered by the organization's credentialing process. To help ensure the proper credentialing of covering practitioners, hospitals should include a space on the application form for practitioners to indicate the names and contact information of practitioners who cover for them on weekends and at other times.

Improvement Tip for Providing Evidence of Current Competence

As evidence of current competence, surveyors now consider several sources of peer recommendations for each LIP. Among them are

- the organization's performance improvement committee, the majority of whose members are the applicant's peers;
- a reference letter or documented telephone conversation about the applicant from a peer who is a member of the hospital's medical staff or who is from outside the hospital, but knowledgeable about the applicant's competence;
- a department or major clinical service chairperson who is a peer; and
- the medical staff executive committee, the majority of whose members are the applicant's peers.

Finally, clinical privileges must be individual-specific. For example, one orthopedist is granted the privilege of performing hand surgery. Another, whose training and experience did not include specialized training in hand surgery, is not granted the privileges. After an applicant is appointed to the medical staff and/or is granted clinical privileges, his or her continued competence must be assured on a continuing basis, a process described in Chapter 5.

REFERENCES

1. Greene J: Growing number of locum tenens doctors strive for simpler life. *AMNews,* Jan 29, 2001.
2. Darr K: Credentialing: The special problem of *locum tenens* physicians. *Hospital Topics,* Sept-Nov 2001.

Example 4-1

Request for Clinical Privileges—Orthopedic Surgery

Memorial Hospital
Fremont, OH 43420

REQUEST FOR CLINICAL PRIVILEGES   **ORTHOPEDIC SURGERY**

Practitioner Name: _____

The orthopedic physician may be granted privileges in orthopedic surgery which includes privileges to attend all manner of orthopedic surgery cases on patients of all ages, and to use the hospital facilities to accomplish this.

All applicants must either be board certified at the time of application or have completed an approved orthopedic training program.

A representative, but of necessity not complete, list of orthopedic surgery privileges follows this statement. It is assumed that other medical illnesses and problems of similar complexity will fall within the identified "bundles." These represent those procedures normally taught in orthopedic training programs. Applicants will provide documentation of having satisfactory proficiency from their training program and/or by having been regularly exercising these procedures at past and present hospital affiliations.

It must be recognized that ill patients do not always fit into a diagnostic category. The ability to make a diagnosis is the province of all physicians. When a physician needs assistance to either make a diagnosis or carry out a specific therapeutic or diagnostic procedure, that physician will obtain appropriate consultation.

Applicants not wishing to apply for privileges listed under a specific "bundle" must strike out and initial that privilege.

Applicants need note that initial appointment and reappointment will be based on a system of performance appraisal. This performance appraisal will utilize information regarding clinical activity and from monitoring and evaluation activities.

Applicants must certify at the time of initial appointment and reappointment, that there are no problems of health or mental status which will interfere with the exercise of clinical privileges requested.

REQUESTED	APPROVED	TABLED*	DENIED
☐ **BASIC ORTHOPEDIC SURGERY PRIVILEGES** Admit patients with orthopedic-related problems Provide consultation for orthopedic-related problems Order diagnostic tests and procedures related to orthopedic problems Treat patients with orthopedic problems	☐	☐	☐
☐ **ANESTHESIA** Local infiltration anesthesia Topical anesthetic application Minor peripheral nerve blocks Conscious sedation	☐	☐	☐
☐ **LARGE JOINT REPLACEMENT** Shoulder Hip Knee	☐	☐	☐

Page 1 of 3

(continued on next page)

SOURCE: Memorial Hospital, Fremont, OH. Used with permission.

EXAMPLES

Request for Clinical Privileges—Orthopedic Surgery (continued)

Memorial Hospital
Fremont, OH 43420

REQUEST FOR CLINICAL PRIVILEGES   **ORTHOPEDIC SURGERY**

Practitioner Name:

REQUESTED	APPROVED	TABLED*	DENIED
☐ **OPERATIVE AND NON-OPERATIVE TREATMENT**	☐	☐	☐

Spine
Pelvis
Upper Extremities
Lower Extremities

Which includes the following, within each anatomic area:
Fractures
Dislocations
Arthritis
Internal derangements
Infections
Tumors
Metabolic diseases of bones
Problems involving trauma and non-traumatic conditions of joints, soft tissue, fascia, bursa, muscles, nerves

	APPROVED	TABLED*	DENIED
☐ **SMALL JOINT SURGERY** (Hand Surgery)	☐	☐	☐
☐ **ARTHROSCOPE**	☐	☐	☐

Practitioners requesting spine surgery procedures must have completed a spine surgery fellowship or performed the procedures requested within the past three (3) years. Attach documentation to support these privilege requests.

	APPROVED	TABLED*	DENIED
☐ **CERVICAL SPINE**	☐	☐	☐

Anterior
    Cervical fusion
    Corpectomy
    Diskectomy, decompression
    Instrumentation
Posterior
    Decompression
    Fusion
    Instrumentation

	APPROVED	TABLED*	DENIED
☐ **THORACIC SPINE**	☐	☐	☐

Anterior
    Corpectomy
    Decompression
    Fusion
    Instrumentation
Posterior
    Decompression
    Fusion
    Instrumentation

Page 2 of 3

(continued on next page)

Request for Clinical Privileges—Orthopedic Surgery (continued)

Memorial Hospital
Fremont, OH 43420

REQUEST FOR CLINICAL PRIVILEGES   **ORTHOPEDIC SURGERY**

Practitioner Name: _____

REQUESTED		APPROVED	TABLED*	DENIED
☐	**APPLICATION OF TONG OR HALO TRACTION**	☐	☐	☐
☐	**LUMBAR/SACRAL SPINE**	☐	☐	☐

Anterior
    Decompression, diskectomy
    Fusion
    Instrumentation
Posterior
    Decompression, diskectomy
    Fusion
    Instrumentation

		APPROVED	TABLED*	DENIED
	INVASIVE			
☐	Discography	☐	☐	☐
☐	Laser assisted spinal endoscopy (LASE)	☐	☐	☐
☐	Myelography	☐	☐	☐
	SURGICAL ASSIST			
☐	My patients only	☐	☐	☐
☐	Emergency cases only	☐	☐	☐
☐	Other (specify) _____	☐	☐	☐
	OTHER			
☐	_____	☐	☐	☐
☐	_____	☐	☐	☐
☐	_____	☐	☐	☐

Does your malpractice policy cover the above privilege request?   Yes   No

TABLED* means: Action on request is pending further documentation of training, experience, etc.

PRIVILEGES REQUESTED BY:

_____
Practitioner Signature   Date

surgery\privilege.ort
9/99

EXAMPLES

Example 4-2

Delineation of Privileges—Surgery

DELINEATION OF PRIVILEGES
GENERAL SURGERY

Revised Date: December 8, 1992

Revised and approved by Credentials Committee: July 3, 2001
Revised and approved by Medical Staff: July 10, 2001

*   Due to reporting requirements under the National Practitioner Data Bank, please request **ONLY** those privileges you intend to exercise and for which you can document education, training and experience.

Privileges in general surgery may be granted to a physician, M.D. or D.O., who has completed an approved residency in general surgery or has education, training and experience equivalent to that of a general surgery residency trained physician for the specific privileges/procedures requested.

DEFINITION OF GENERAL SURGERY PRIVILEGES:
A surgeon is a physician trained in the understanding of wound healing, hemostasis, hematologic disorders, oncology, shock, circulatory physiology, surgical microbiology, respiratory physiology, gastrointestinal physiology, GU physiology, surgical endocrinology, surgical nutrition, fluid and electrolyte balance, metabolic response to injury including burns, musculoskeletal body mechanics and physiology, immunobiology, and transplantation for all ages and both genders. Applied surgical anatomy and surgical pathology. The surgeon is skilled in pre-operative, operative, and post-operative care for patients; specifically diseases of the head and neck, breasts, skin and soft tissues, alimentary track, abdomen, vascular system, endocrine system, comprehensive management of trauma and emergency operations, and surgical critical care.

Training includes the use of rigid and flexible endoscopy procedures, such as sigmoidoscopy, colonoscopy, upper endoscopy, laparoscopy, laryngoscopy, bronchoscopy, and fine needle aspiration.

Training in the evolving diagnostic and therapeutic modalities such as laser.

The surgeon is skilled in emergency room management and stabilization of patients with surgical conditions. In addition to operative care, the surgeon is trained in the non-operative care of conditions of a surgical nature.

(continued on next page)

SOURCE: DeKalb Memorial Hospital, Auburn, IN. Used with permission.

Delineation of Privileges—Surgery (continued)

DEKALB ✚ MEMORIAL

General Surgery Delineation of Privileges   **Page: 2**

DELINEATION OF PRIVILEGES
GENERAL SURGERY

Privileges will include the ability to admit, work-up and provide services including consultation and performance of procedures granted relative to this area.

Adrenal procedures	Appendectomy	Biliary reconstruction
Biliary tract and pancreatic surgery	Breast biopsy	Breast surgery greater than biopsy (lumpectomy, mastectomy)
Chest wall surgery	Cuticular lesions, excision	Diaphragmatic procedures
Esophageal procedures	Gall bladder surgery, **open**	Head & Neck surgery deeper than the Platysma
Hemorrhoidectomy, simple	Hemorrhoids, complicated	Hernia, abdominal, larger (> 6cm)
Hernia, diaphragmatic	Hernia, ventral	Herniorrhaphy, inguinal
I&D Abscess	Liver and spleen surgery for biopsy or traumatic splenectomy	Liver, larger resection
Non-body cavity entering biopsy	Parathyroid surgery	Peripheral vascular cutdown
Pilonidal cyst excision	Splenorraphy	Stomach, bowel, colon surgery
Subcutaneous cysts and tumors	T&A	Thyroid, FNA
Thyroid, nodules/cyst excision	Thyroidectomy, partial	Thyroidectomy, total
Vein surgery in the legs		

ENDOSCOPIC PROCEDURES

Bronchoscopy	Colonoscopy	Endoscopic biopsy
Endoscopic cautery	Endoscopic injection therapy	Endoscopic polypectomy
Esophageal dilatation	Esophagogastroscopy	Laryngoscopy, flexible
Peritoneoscopy	Percutaneous endoscopic gastrostomy	Sigmoidoscopy, flexible
Sigmoidoscopy, rigid		

LAPAROSCOPIC PROCEDURES

Appendectomy	Cholecystectomy	Gastric resection/repair/Nissen
Hernia	Intra-abdominal organ (solid)	Intestinal resection/repair

(continued on next page)

113

Delineation of Privileges—Surgery (continued)

DEKALB MEMORIAL

General Surgery Delineation of Privileges

Page: 3

REQUEST FOR
SPECIAL PRIVILEGES

NOTE: Special privileges and procedures require education, training and experience commensurate with the privileges and procedures requested.

Amputation, major	Casting and splinting	Fractures, open reduction and internal fixation
Ganglion excision	Tendon repair, extensor	Tendon repair, flexor
Aortic aneurysm	Carotid endarterectomy	Chest Surgery
Mediastinal procedure	Mediastinoscopy	Peripheral vascular procedure
Surgery involving lung and pleura, including lobectomy, pneumonectomy & segmentectomy	Laparoscopic Thoracic surgery	Colposcopy with and without biopsy
C-section	Cystostomy	Cystectomy, partial
D&C	Laparoscopic surgery of Gynecological organs	Hysterectomy, abdominal
Hysterectomy, vaginal	Laparoscopic Tubal ligation, LTD	
Tubal ligation, LTD	Tubal ligation, mini-laparotomy	Oophorectomy
Salpingectomy	Tubal ligation, post-partum	Vaginoplasty
Vulvar biopsy	Circumcision	Nephrectomy
Scrotal & testicle procedures	Ureter repair	Urethropexy
Urinary bladder repair	Vasectomy	Laser, use of surgical
Myringotomy	Sentinel Lymph Node biopsy *with* axillary dissection	Sentinel Lymph Node biopsy *without* axillary dissection
	Harmonic Scalpel	

Minimal Sedation (anxiolysis) - a drug induced state during which patients respond normally to verbal commands. Although cognitive function and coordination may be impaired, ventilatory and cardiovascular functions are unaffected.

Moderate Sedation/Analgesia (conscious sedation) - a drug induced depression of consciousness during which the patients response purposefully to verbal commands, either alone or accompanied by light tactile stimulation. No interventions are required to maintain a patent airway and spontaneous ventilation is adequate. Cardiovascular function is usually maintained.

Deep Sedation/Analgesia -- a drug induced depression of consciousness during which patients cannot be easily aroused but response purposefully following repeated or painful stimulation. The ability to independently maintain ventilatory function may be impaired. Patients may require assistance in maintaining a patent airway and spontaneous ventilation may be inadequate. Cardiovascular function is usually maintained.

(continued on next page)

Delineation of Privileges—Surgery (continued)

DEKALB MEMORIAL HOSPITAL INC

General Surgery Delineation of Privileges   **Page: 4**

Other privileges as requested: (please list all other requested privileges, and only those that can be performed at D.M.H.)

_____   _____
Applicant's signature   Date

_____   _____
Credentials Committee   Date

Date approved by Medical Executive Committee: _____

Date approved by Board of Directors: _____

EXAMPLES

Example 4-3

Department of the Navy. General Surgery—Core Privileges

DEPARTMENT OF THE NAVY
General Surgery - Core Privileges

- Comprehensive general surgery examinations, consultation, diagnosis, and treatment planning
- Operational medicine and primary care medicine core privileges

Assessment with operative or nonoperative treatment of:

- Trauma
- Wounds and conditions of soft tissue including aspiration, biopsy, and repair
- Cysts and abscesses to include aspiration and incision and drainage
- Conditions involving the thyroid, parathyroid, and adrenal gland
- Condition of the ovary and testis
- Abdominal wall hernias
- Tumors, congenital, and inflammatory diseases of the gastrointestinal tract
- Tumors, congenital, and inflammatory diseases of the liver and biliary tract
- Breast conditions to include aspiration, biopsy, and evaluation
- Abdominal wall hernias
- Peptic and duodenal ulcer disease
- Varicose veins

Procedures:

- Insertion of monitoring catheters and intravenous lines
- Skin grafting
- Nerve and artery biopsy
- Lymph node biopsy or excision
- Tracheostomy
- Thoracentesis
- Radical, modified radical, total, and segmental mastectomies
- Paracentesis, peritoneal lavage, endoscopy with or without biopsy
- Gastrotomy and gastrostomy
- Hemorrhoidectomy, fissurectomy, fistulectomy, and sphincterotomy
- Exploratory laparotomy
- Ostomy formation and management

(continued on next page)

SOURCE: American Health Information Management Association. Used with permission.

Department of the Navy. General Surgery—Core Privileges (continued)

- Drainage of intraperitoneal abscess
- Internal hernia including diaphragmatic
- Splenectomy and splenorrhaphy
- Tube thoracostomy
- Pericardiocentesis
- Repair of wound disruptions
- Major and minor amputations
- Radical groin and axillary dissection with or without removal of limb
- Appendectomy

General Surgery - Supplemental Privileges

____ Insertion of pacemaker wires

____ Burn care

____ Assessment and treatment of tumors, congenital and inflammatory conditions of the mouth, face, and throat

____ Repair and reconstruction of vascular abnormalities, injuries, or diseases (includes placement of vascular grafts and arterioplasties)

____ Endoscopic dilation or sphincterotomy

____ Colonoscopy and upper gastrointestinal endoscopy, with or without biopsy

____ Cranial burr holes

____ Excision of salivary glands

____ Esophageal resection

____ Radical neck dissection

____ Partial hepatectomy, segmentectomy, and lobectomy

____ Pancreatectomy and other pancreatic surgery

____ Vena cava interruption, sympathectomy

____ Pleural abrasion and pleurectomy

____ Pulmonary wedge resection and pulmonary lobectomy

____ Pneumonectomy

____ Portacaval or other shunt

____ Intravenous conscious sedation

____ Laparoendoscopy with or without biopsy

____ Basic laparoendoscopic operative procedures to include:

    ____ Cholecystectomy

    ____ Herniorrhaphy (ventral or inguinal)

(continued on next page)

EXAMPLES

EXAMPLES

Department of the Navy. General Surgery—Core Privileges (continued)

_____ Appendectomy

_____ Advanced laparoendoscopic operative procedures to include:

    _____ Intestinal resection with or without anastomosis

    _____ Nissen fundoplication

    _____ Vagotomy, seromyotomy, pyloromyotomy, or pyloroplasty

    _____ Common bile duct exploration

    _____ Splenectomy

Other:

Treatment Facility: _____   Date Requested: _____

Practitioner Name: _____   Date Approved: _____

EXAMPLES

Example 4-4

University Hospitals of Cleveland, Department of Family Medicine, Requirements for Specialized Procedures

University Hospitals Health System

University Hospitals of Cleveland

DEPARTMENT OF FAMILY MEDICINE REQUIREMENTS FOR SPECIALIZED PROCEDURES page 1 of 3

Privileges to perform specialized procedures, those marked with an asterisk (*) on the privilege delineation form, may be granted to those candidates who meet the requirements for training and/or experience. Please review and choose the area(s) which applies to you.

SPECIALIZED PROCEDURES	ALL APPLICANTS (WHO DO NOT CURRENTLY HOLD LISTED PRIVILEGES) - APPOINTMENT AND REAPPOINTMENT	ALL REAPPOINTMENT APPLICANTS WHO CURRENTLY HOLD LISTED PRIVILEGES ★
Colposcopy with endocervical curettage and cervical biopsy w/wo cervical cryosurgery Vasectomy	Provide a letter of recommendation from the supervising physician of your primary hospital. The letter should verify your training, sufficient experience and current competence (past 2 years) to perform each procedure requested.	No additional requirement. ★ If you are requesting additional specialized procedures, please refer to instructions in columns 1 and 2.
Loop electrical excision procedure	Choose I or II (select one) I. Provide a course certificate (or a letter from the course presenter) attesting that you have satisfactorily completed a CME category I course that includes hands-on experience. The certificate (or letter) must indicate the date of the course and the hours of didactic versus hands-on training; <u>and</u> Demonstrate competence by being proctored for a minimum of five (5) cases. The proctor must be a member of the Medical Staff of UHC with admitting and clinical privileges to perform the procedure. If expertise is unavailable at UHC, an appropriate proctor may be chosen from another institution. The proctor must make a written recommendation to the Medical Staff Credentialing Department attesting to your competence. Privileges will be granted only after this requirement is met. or II. Provide a letter of recommendation from your residency/ fellowship training director verifying your sufficient training ,experience (volume) and competence to perform the procedure requested; <u>and</u> Provide a <u>case list</u> as evidence that you have performed a minimum of five (5) cases during the previous two years. Please note the indications, outcomes, and complications for each case.	Provide a <u>case list</u> (form attached) of Loop electrical excision procedures. The list should note procedures performed, indications, outcomes and complications.

(continued on next page)

SOURCE: University Hospitals Health System, University Hospitals of Cleveland. Department of Family Medicine and Medical Staff Credentialing and Information Management. Cleveland, OH. Used with permission.

EXAMPLES

University Hospitals of Cleveland, Department of Family Medicine, Requirements for Specialized Procedures (continued)

University Hospitals Health System

University Hospitals of Cleveland

DEPARTMENT OF FAMILY MEDICINE REQUIREMENTS FOR SPECIALIZED PROCEDURES page 2 of 3

SPECIALIZED PROCEDURES	ALL APPLICANTS (WHO DO NOT CURRENTLY HOLD LISTED PRIVILEGES) - APPOINTMENT AND REAPPOINTMENT	ALL REAPPOINTMENT APPLICANTS WHO CURRENTLY HOLD LISTED PRIVILEGES ★
Acupuncture	Provide a course certificate (or a letter from the course presenter) attesting that you have satisfactorily completed a course in medical acupuncture sponsored by a recognized training institution. The certificate (or letter) must indicate the date of the course and the hours of training. Note: Those who have completed a residency/fellowship training program that included training in medical acupuncture have already met this requirement. Documented proof of training in the form of a letter of recommendation is required.	No additional requirement. ★ If you are requesting additional specialized procedures, please refer to instructions in columns 1 and 2.
Naso-pharyngoscopy (flexible)	Provide a course certificate (or a letter from the course presenter) attesting that you have satisfactorily completed a CME category I course that includes hands-on experience. The certificate (or letter) must indicate the date of the course and the hours of didactic versus hands-on training; Note: Those who have complete a residency or fellowship training program which includes naso-pharyngoscopy (flexible) have already met this requirement. Documented proof of training required.	No additional requirement. ★ If you are requesting additional specialized procedures, please refer to instructions in columns 1 and 2.
Family Medicine OB/GYN	I. Provide a letter of recommendation from the supervising physician of your primary hospital. The letter should verify at least 3 months of OB/GYN training during residency/fellowship, sufficient experience (volume) and current competence (within past 2 years) to perform each procedure requested. and II. Provide a case list (form attached) of OB/GYN procedures. Include the following, if applicable: spontaneous vaginal delivery (cephalic presentation), vacuum-assisted and outlet forceps deliveries; repair of third and fourth degree lacerations; dilatation and curettage; and pregnancy terminations. The list should note procedure performed, indications, outcomes and complications.	Provide a case list (form attached) of OB/GYN procedures. Include the following, if applicable: spontaneous vaginal delivery (cephalic presentation), vacuum-assisted and outlet forceps deliveries; repair of third and fourth degree lacerations; dilatation and curettage; and pregnancy terminations. The list should note procedure performed, indications, outcomes and complications.

(continued on next page)

120

University Hospitals of Cleveland, Department of Family Medicine, Requirements for Specialized Procedures (continued)

UniversityHospitals HealthSystem
University Hospitals of Cleveland

DEPARTMENT OF FAMILY MEDICINE REQUIREMENTS FOR SPECIALIZED PROCEDURES page 3 of 3

LIST OF OBSTETRIC AND GYNECOLOGIC PROCEDURES

Candidate's Name _____

Date	Patient ID and Hospital #	Indicate: Supervising, Performing or Assisting	Procedure(s)	Complications or Comments

EXAMPLES

Example 4-5

Peer Cover Letter for Medical Staff Appointment and Privileges

MEMORIAL
H O S P I T A L

715 SOUTH TAFT AVENUE
FREMONT, OHIO 43420
419-332-7321

*[DATE]

#[REF_NAME]
#[REF_ADDRS]
#[REF_CITY], #[REF_STATE] #[REF_ZIP]

Re: #[FIRSTNAME] #[LASTNAME], #[DEGREE]
Specialty: #[SPECIALTY1]

Dear Doctor:

The above referenced practitioner is applying for appointment to the Medical Staff at Memorial Hospital. Dr. #[LASTNAME] has listed you as a professional reference. Please assist us in evaluating the practitioner by submitting a professional letter of evaluation. Said letter should attest to the practitioner's current clinical competence, performance of clinical judgment and technical skills, ethical character, physical and emotional health status, and ability to work cooperatively with others.

A copy of the release and immunity statement executed by the practitioner which constitutes consent to this inquiry and to your response is enclosed. A return envelope is also enclosed for your convenience, or you may fax your letter to my attention at 419-334-6602.

Thank you for your assistance in our evaluation of the practitioner. All information will be held in the strictest confidence and will be used only by those individuals involved in the credentialing process.

Sincerely,

Denise K. Woolley, CMSC, CPCS
Director, Medical Staff Services

SOURCE: Memorial Hospital, Fremont, OH. Used with permission.

Example 4-6

Credentialing Worksheet

UHHS Bedford Medical Center
CREDENTIALING WORKSHEET

Coordinators Initials: _____
Pre-Application Received: ☐ YES ☐ NO

Applicant: _____
Department/Specialty: _____

Date Application Rec'd: _____
Date Process Completed : _____

( ) License (Expires:)	( ) CME Log	( ) Release Form	( ) NRP (Exp:)
( ) DEA (Expires:)	( ) ECFMG	( ) Delineation	( ) BTLS/ATLS (Exp:)
( ) Insurance (Expires:)	( ) UPIN	( ) Curriculum Vitae	( ) BCLS/ACLS (Exp)
( ) Academic Certificates	( ) Photograph	( ) Medicaid #	( ) Corporate Compliance Certificate
( ) App Fee (ck#:)	( ) Rct of Bylaws	( ) Medicare #	( ) TB Test Results ( )
( ) Conscious Sedation Criteria (Score:)	Other:		

VERIFICATIONS		DATE SENT	SOURCE USED	DATE REC'D
State Licenses:	OHIO		OSMB Website	
AMA/AOA PROFILE			AMA Website	
NATIONAL PRACTITIONER DATA BANK REPORT			Cactus/NPDB	
OFFICE OF INSPECTOR GENERAL REPORT			OIG Website	
ECFMG #				
Board Certification:	☐YES ☐NO ☐YES ☐NO			
Malpractice Carrier:				
		DATES		
Medical/Dental School:				
Internship:				
Residency:				
Fellowship:				
Hospital Affiliations:				
Peer References:				
Miscellaneous:				

☐ Temporary Privileges Granted: _____ Expire: _____
Information needed from Applicant (Letter sent - ☐ YES ☐ NO)

_____
_____

Originals/verification worksheet

SOURCE: UHHS Bedford Medical Center, Bedford, OH. Used with permission.

Example 4-7

Department Chair Initial Appointment Assessment/Recommendation Form

UHHS BEDFORD MEDICAL STAFF
INITIAL APPOINTMENT ASSESSMENT/RECOMMENDATIONS

NAME:	
SPECIALTY:	
STAFF CATEGORY:	

Department Chair Assessment
Indicate that each item has been reviewed by placing a " √ " in the reviewed box.

	REVIEWED		REVIEWED
APPLICATION FORM		HOSPITAL AFFILIATIONS	
PRIVILEGES REQUESTED		PEER REFERENCES	
CONTINUING EDUCATION		NPDB REPORT	
CLAIMS HISTORY		LICENSURE VERIFICATION	
EDUCATION		OIG REPORT	
ECFMG (if applicable)		Other:	

Please complete the following evaluation based on personal knowledge and the information contained within the initial appointment profile.

	FAVORABLE	UNFAVORABLE	NOT ASSESSED
Medical Knowledge & Clinical Competence			
Professional Judgement			
Ability to work with others			
Citizenship, Compliance with Bylaws			
Medical Record Completion/Quality			
Physician/patient relationship			

	YES	NO	NOT ASSESSED
Is there any evidence of physical or mental disability, including possible dependence on drugs or alcohol, which would prevent this physician from carrying out his/her responsibilities to his/her patients?			
Is there any privilege being requested by the applicant for which he/she does not possess the necessary skills and experience to perform appropriately?			
Does the information contained in the applicant's claims history indicate any cause for further review/proctoring?			

If you answered "unfavorable" or "yes" to any of the above questions, please explain below:

_____

_____

_____

(continued on next page)

Department Chair Initial Appointment Assessment/Recommendation Form (continued)

RECOMMENDATIONS: NAME: _____

	Appointment to the Medical Staff with no restrictions.
	Staff Category recommended: _____
	Appointment to the Medical Staff with the following restrictions: _____ _____
	Appointment to the Medical Staff be denied for the following reasons: _____ _____

Department Chair Comments & Approval	_____ _____ _____ _____ _____ Signature Date
COMMITTEE COMMENTS (if any)	_____ _____ _____ _____ _____
APPROVAL DATES	CREDENTIALS COMMITTEE: _____ MEDICAL EXECUTIVE COMMITTEE: _____ BOARD OF TRUSTEES: _____

ceckley\appointment information\approval form

EXAMPLES

EXAMPLES

Example 4-8

Proctorship Program Surgical

PROCTORSHIP PROGRAM SURGICAL

DATE OF THIS REVIEW: _____

☐ Direct/Concurrent Review
☐ Retrospective Chart Review

INDIVIDUAL PROCTORED: _____   PHYSICIAN INDEX #: _____

PROCTOR: _____   PHYSICIAN INDEX #: _____

DIAGNOSIS: _____   PROCEDURE: _____

EVALUATE IN TERMS OF COMPLETENESS AND ACCURACY		ACCEPTABLE	MARGINAL* EXPLAIN*	UNACCEPTABLE* EXPLAIN*	N/A
I. PRE-OPERATIVE WORK UP:					
H & P ARE COMPLETE/ACCURATE	1.	☐	☐	☐	☐
CONSENT(S) APPROPRIATE/SIGNED	2.	☐	☐	☐	☐
LAB AND X-RAY ARE APPROPRIATE	3.	☐	☐	☐	☐
INDICATIONS FOR PROCEDURE	4.	☐	☐	☐	☐
II. INTRAOPERATIVE PHASE:					
SURGICAL TECHNIQUE:					
MANUAL DEXTERITY, APPROACH TO PROCEDURE	4.	☐	☐	☐	☐
MANAGEMENT OF ANY COMPLICATIONS	5.	☐	☐	☐	☐
SURGICAL JUDGMENT:					
COMPLETENESS AND DEGREE/EXTENT OF RESECTION; DEGREE TO WHICH OPERATION CONFORMS TO ACCEPTED PRACTICES	6.	☐	☐	☐	☐
ACCURACY OF DIAGNOSIS:					
PRE-OP DX COMPARES WITH POST-OP	7.	☐	☐	☐	☐
PROCEDURES APPROPRIATE TO CONSENT SIGNED	8.	☐	☐	☐	☐
SURGERY JUSTIFIED BY THE FINDINGS	9.	☐	☐	☐	☐
III. RETROSPECTIVE OBSERVATIONS:					
OPERATIVE REPORTS/PROGRESS NOTES ARE APPROPRIATE AND TIMELY	10.	☐	☐	☐	☐
CHART REFLECTS DISCHARGE PLANS, INCLUDING INSTRUCTIONS TO THE PATIENT	11.	☐	☐	☐	☐
LENGTH OF STAY WITHIN ACCEPTED STANDARDS	12.	☐	☐	☐	☐
COMPLICATIONS APPROPRIATELY DOCUMENTED AND MANAGED	13.	☐	☐	☐	☐
SURGERY WAS JUSTIFIED BY THE PATH REPORTS	14.	☐	☐	☐	☐
IV. OVERALL PERFORMANCE:					
INTERACTION WITH COLLEAGUES AND STAFF	15.	☐	☐	☐	☐
APPROPRIATE USE OF CONSULTANTS	16.	☐	☐	☐	☐
INTERACTIONS WITH PATIENT	17.	☐	☐	☐	☐
CARE PROVIDED MEETS COMMUNITY STANDARDS	18.	☐	☐	☐	☐

IS THERE ANY ASPECT OF THIS PATIENT'S TREATMENT AND FOLLOW-UP WITH WHICH YOU ARE UNEASY OR

UNCOMFORTABLE: ☐ NO   ☐ IF YES, PLEASE EXPLAIN: _____

_____

GENERAL OVERALL IMPRESSION OF THE CARE PROVIDED: _____

_____

_____

_____   _____

Proctor's Signature   Date   Chair's Signature   Date

*Please explain on the reverse side of this form any marginal or unacceptable evaluations. The Department Chair shall provide a copy of this report to the individual proctored.

SOURCE: University of California Davis Health System, Sacramento, CA. Used with permission.

CHAPTER 5

Continuing Competence Assessment of Licensed Independent Practitioners

This chapter addresses continuing competence assessment of licensed independent practitioners (LIPs) covered by the Medical Staff standards. It details how hospitals ensure the competence of LIPs from the notice of acceptance to the medical staff and/or delineation of clinical privileges through regular and continuing assessment of competence at specified intervals. For LIPs, that period of time is at least every two years, concurrent with reappraisal, reappointment, and renewal activities.

The reappraisal, reappointment, and renewal of clinical privileges are steps in the process of continuing medical staff membership and privileges. Reappraisal relates to the review and evaluation of adherence to medical staff membership requirements and performance of clinical privileges; it leads to a decision regarding reappointment and renewal. Reappointment refers to the individual's appointment or status of medical staff membership, and renewal refers to clinical privileges.

The ultimate goal of the reappraisal, reappointment, and renewal of clinical privileges process is to ensure good patient care by certifying that clinicians are competent. The process
- identifies good performance;
- identifies potential issues or concerns for groups of practitioners as well as individuals;

- focuses on education rather than censure; and
- provides for the limitation or removal of membership or clinical privileges as a last resort.

The methods used to verify current competence during the initial privilege or appointment granting process are significantly different than those used to verify continuing competence. For a new applicant, the hospital must obtain verification information from outside its scope of control. Applicants must prove their worthiness for privileges and appointment. For reappraisal and renewal, however, the burden of proof shifts to the hospital, which must prove that individuals either continue to be qualified or are no longer qualified to hold their clinical privileges at the current (or increased) level. A majority (and often all) of data used during the evaluation process is generally provided from within the organization.

The continuing competence assessment process through reappraisal, reappointment, and renewal includes the following activities:
- LIPs who wish to continue to provide care or services in or for the hospital apply for reappointment to the medical staff and/or renewal or revision of clinical privileges. For reappointment to the medical staff and/or to have their privileges renewed, they supply information related to current competence.

- Medical staff leaders collect and assess information about the applicant's current ability to continue to perform up to defined expectations and the requested clinical privileges.
- Medical staff leaders make a decision to grant or deny medical staff reappointment and to renew or revise clinical privileges, delineating the privileges granted and outlining any limitations or conditions.
- Medical staff department directors ensure continuing surveillance of the professional performance of all LIPs with delineated clinical privileges.

A detailed description of each activity follows the discussion of JCAHO requirements.

JCAHO Requirements

A hospital's bylaws, rules and regulations, and policies and procedures outline the process for reappointment to the medical staff and that of granting and renewing or revising hospital-specific clinical privileges. These documents describe the applicant's responsibilities, the medical staff's method of evaluation and recommendation, and the governing body's authority to reappoint the individual and to grant, renew, or revise clinical privileges. The governing body is the ultimate authority and must exercise this responsibility without arbitrariness, capriciousness, discrimination, or conflict with the bylaws. Appropriate care must be taken whether an affirmative or adverse decision is rendered.

The reappraisal, reappointment, and renewal of clinical privileges include the following activities:
- The LIP applies for membership and requests clinical privileges.
- The hospital gathers data and reports.
- The hospital evaluates the information and makes a decision.

These activities require that the following conditions be met:

- Medical staff members and all others who have delineated clinical privileges must abide by medical staff and departmental bylaws, rules and regulations, and policies and are subject to evaluation as part of the organization's performance improvement activities.
- Departmental directors are responsible for overseeing the professional performance of all department staff who have delineated clinical privileges.
- Appointment or reappointment to the medical staff and the initial granting, renewing, or revision of clinical privileges also are based on information about the applicant's competence.
- The mechanism for granting, renewing, or revising clinical privileges ensures that the privileges granted are hospital specific and based on the individual's demonstrated current competence.
- Mechanisms exist to address adverse decisions pertaining to renewal, revocation, or revision of clinical privileges.
- Mechanisms may differ for medical staff members and other staff who hold clinical privileges.
- Decisions on reappointments, revocation, or renewal of clinical privileges are subject to a fair hearing and appeal process.
- The bylaws, rules, regulations, and policies of the medical staff mandate that the applicant for reappointment or renewal of clinical privileges be required to submit proof of current ability to perform privileges.
- Privileges are based on the available conclusions drawn from organization performance-improvement activities.
- The medical staff, in making recommendations for appointment or termination, and for the initial granting, revising, or revoking of clinical privileges, bases its decision, in part, on information provided by a peer of the applicant.
- Departmental or major clinical service recommendations are part of the basis for making recommendations for continued membership on the medical staff or for delineating individual clinical privileges.

- Reappointment to the medical staff and the renewal or revision of clinical privileges is based on the continuous monitoring of information about the individual's professional performance, judgment, clinical, or technical skills.
- Decisions on reappointments, revocation, revision, or renewal of clinical privileges must be based on criteria that are related directly to the quality of care.
- Medical staff plays a lead role in organizational performance improvement activities when assessment process findings are relevant to an individual's performance; staff determines their use in peer review or the continuing evaluations of an LIP's competence, in accordance with the standards on renewing or revising clinical privileges delineated in this chapter.
- All staff who have delineated clinical privileges must participate in continuing education.
- Staff's participation in continuing education is documented, and is considered in decisions on reappointment, renewal, or revision of individual clinical privileges.
- Medical records are continually reviewed for completeness and timeliness, and action is taken to improve the quality and timeliness of documentation that affects patient care.

The Application Process

Each applicant for reappointment and renewal or revision of clinical privileges completes an application that includes the following information determined by the hospital:
- Previously successful or currently pending challenges to any licensure or registration (for example, state, district, Drug Enforcement Administration) or voluntary relinquishment of such licensure or registration;
- Voluntary or involuntary termination of medical staff membership or voluntary or involuntary limitation, reduction, or loss of clinical privileges at another health care organization;

- Involvement in a professional liability action under circumstances specified in the medical staff bylaws, rules and regulations, and policies;
- Final judgments or settlements in a professional liability action;
- Request for renewal or revision of clinical privileges;
- Documentation of participation in continuing medical education (CME), per hospital policy or regulation;
- A statement of ability to perform;
- An agreement to abide by the bylaws, rules and regulations, and policies and procedures;
- Consent to review records and documents pertinent to licensure, training or experience, current competence, and ability to perform; and
- Any other elements required by the hospital's bylaws.

Any statement regarding the applicant's health should be confirmed by at least a countersignature by a department director in a departmentalized hospital or the chief of staff in a non-departmentalized hospital. Because the amount of information requested of the applicant may become burdensome or even confusing, some hospitals assist the practitioner by providing a checklist on the last page of the reapplication form. This tool assists the practitioner in ensuring that all items requested are being submitted and reduces the burden on the hospital staff to send second requests for information that may have been inadvertently omitted.

There are several routes for requesting renewal or revision of privileges. Some hospitals choose to have practitioners request new privileges at each reappraisal cycle. With this approach, the LIP receives a copy of current clinical privileges along with a blank privilege form to complete.

Correspondence requesting that practitioners ask for only the clinical privileges that they plan to use accompanies this material.

Practitioners are often reluctant to give up clinical privileges—even if the privileges have not been exercised for several years. Some hospitals also provide a printout of the cases treated or procedures performed during the preceding two years to influence self-limiting decisions. This approach helps the practitioner relate past practice to current competence and future practice.

For instance, in the case of a practitioner who has not performed certain procedures for some time, the individual may not choose to request the same scope of procedures for the coming two-year period. Under this circumstance, neither the practitioner nor the organization need report the reduction to the NPDB unless the practitioner has been accused of professional incompetence or improper professional conduct by a health care entity and has surrendered the privilege in return for the accusing entity's promise not to pursue an investigation into the incompetence or impropriety. Reductions in privileges need only be reported to the NPDB in instances in which professional competence or conduct is in question. The practitioner's decision not to request clinical privileges may be based on the lack of current experience with the privilege/procedure, a self-limitation of scope of practice, or the cost of professional liability insurance. If the practitioner cannot demonstrate current competence, the hospital has the option of granting the privilege under the condition that the LIP be supervised, or it may impose alternative methods for demonstrating competence for the privileges that remain.

The second method of renewing or revising privilege requests involves using a form such as that shown in Example 5-1, Biennial Application for 2001-2003 Reappointment and Renewal of Clinical Privileges, pages 137–138. This method also encourages the practitioner to closely evaluate the current level of privileges and modify future requests accordingly. For medical and legal reasons, hospitals that use this method normally require that the original requests be updated periodically.

The Medical Staff Services Department of Memorial Hospital in Fremont, Ohio, provides physicians with a printout of the most up-to-date information in their credentials files and asks each applicant for reappointment/renewed privileges to review, verify and update his or her information, as appropriate. Based on a calendar-year reappointment and renewal of privileges cycle, on August 1 the hospital sends a Request for Reappointment and Renewal of Clinical Privileges document to LIPs whose privileges expire December 31 (see Example 5-2 on pages 139–141). Data used for each section are taken from the credentials master file. A questionnaire on professional liability suits and other matters and the applicant's consent and release form constitute page 2 of the document. Page 3 provides a sign-off sheet for a description of delineated privileges, which is attached.

LIPs have four weeks to verify and amend the information. The organization's medical staff bylaws require LIPs who have appointments and privileges to return the information within a specified number of days of the expiration of privileges. Medical Staff Services Department staff send a reminder, followed by a certified letter, if the practitioners do not return the material promptly.

Gathering and Evaluating Competence-Related Data

The hospital's reappraisal and renewal process must be based on information regarding the individual's competence. This involves continual monitoring of information concerning the individual's professional performance, judgment, and clinical and/or technical skills.

Competence Criteria

Current competence is determined by
- pertinent results of performance-improvement activities and data gathered during the previous period of clinical privileges;
- peer recommendations;

- the individual's professional performance, clinical judgment, and technical skills in performing procedures, and treating and managing patients;
- outcomes of procedures and treatment performed by the applicant (for example, reviews could encompass outcomes of operative and other procedures, medication and blood usage, and medical records); and
- departmental or major clinical services recommendations.

The evidence base for assessing continuing competence may include experience, outcome analysis, observation of skills, peer review results, peer recommendations, patient satisfaction and complaints, and outcome of performance improvement projects. Additional clinical criteria may be based on utilization-management and risk-management data. Other criteria may include attendance at appropriate meetings, complaints regarding behavior, and failure to abide by administrative rules and regulations. At a minimum, criteria for assessing continuing competence will pertain to evidence of current licensure, current competence, and the practitioner's ability to perform the privileges requested. The following information provided by the applicant in accordance with the hospital's bylaws is also considered: an applicant's loss of staff privileges at an area hospital, licensure loss or relinquishment, involvement in a malpractice suit, and health conditions that would affect performance.

Criteria for Renewing Privileges. Criteria for renewing privileges are often termed maintenance criteria. An example of a maintenance criterion might be requiring the practitioner to have performed certain procedures within the current two-year period of privileges, with the cases reviewed for appropriateness and outcome.

All practitioners who have delineated clinical privileges must participate in continuing medical education (CME). Further, the educational activities must relate, at least in part, to the clinical privileges granted. The specific number of hours required is defined by the organization. The individual's participation in CME is documented and considered in decisions about reappointment and/or renewal or revision of clinical privileges.

Decisions on renewal, revision, or revocation of clinical privileges must be made with consideration of criteria that are directly related to the quality of care. If criteria unrelated to the quality of care or professional competency are used, evidence must be presented that the impact of resultant decisions on the quality of care has been evaluated. As with initial appointments, decisions must not be based on gender, race, creed, or national origin.

Peer Review

Peer review is the concurrent or retrospective review of a health professional's performance of clinical professional activities by peers through formally adopted written procedures that provide for adequate notice and an opportunity for a hearing of the professional under review.[1]

Peer review is often used as a method to obtain information about an LIP's continued competence when his or her performance of a clinical privilege is questioned as a result of the organization's measurement and assessment activities.

Members of the medical staff
- define the circumstances that require peer review;
- specify the participants in the review process;
- outline the time frame for review; and
- define the circumstances under which external peer review is required.

An effectively functioning peer review process is consistent, timely, defensible, balanced, useful, and continuing. Usefulness requires that the results of peer review activities be considered in practitioner-specific credentialing and privileging decisions.

Example 5-3, on pages 142–145, illustrates the peer review policy of Pacific Communities Health District, Newport, Oregon.

Peer Recommendations

Peer recommendations are critical to the assessment of a practitioner's continuing competence. As described in Chapter 4, an acceptable peer recommendation is a recommendation from a professional in the same specialty or professional practice as the applicant, and who has firsthand knowledge of him or her. Sources for peer recommendations may include

- a performance-improvement committee that includes the applicant's peers;
- a reference letter or documented telephone conversation about the applicant from a peer who is knowledgeable about the applicant's competence; and
- a department or major clinical service chairperson who is a peer.

Peer recommendations refer to relevant training or experience, current competence, and how well the applicant fulfilled hospital-specific obligations. The hospital selects the peer, either from within the hospital or outside of it. The peer provides a recommendation based on the applicant's clinical performance, relationships with peers, and ability to relate to patients.

Data Quality

The effectiveness of the reappraisal and renewal of clinical privileges process depends on the quality of the data submitted. The system that provides the data, therefore, is crucial. Input from professionals from multiple areas of the hospital comprises the broad scope of information and resources required. The following individuals contribute to the data on which the reappraisal and renewal of clinical privileges process is based:

- Medical staff representatives;
- Services professionals;
- Performance improvement specialists;
- Risk management specialists;
- Information systems staff;
- Health information management specialists, and
- Nursing and ancillary personnel responsible for clinical pathways or performance improvement activities.

Each hospital determines the information that would be helpful in determining the continuing competence of practitioners.

After a decision has been made about the data that will be provided and by whom, a time line for gathering it is established. The information flows from various individuals responsible for obtaining it.

Because there are so many components to the reappraisal and renewal or revision of privileges process and so many individuals involved, it is often helpful to develop a manual or automated tracking system to identify a practitioner's location in the privileging process.

Data Analysis

Data analysis also varies from hospital to hospital. At some facilities, the data may be given directly to the department or section chair for review, analysis, and recommendation. At others, the information may be evaluated first by individuals from medical staff services and/or the performance improvement departments. In the latter instance, the data may be analyzed and highlighted—either in an informal manner, such as by attaching a color-coded tab to the area of concern, or through a more formal memo that outlines the reviewer's comments.

As the data are analyzed, trends may be revealed. For example, data indicating a high rate of readmissions coupled with a shorter than average length of stay for one practitioner's patients might indicate the need for the practitioner to reconsider the discharge criteria. Other examples could include the following:

- Higher than normal cost per case, coupled with a tendency to use consultants;
- Longer length of stay; or
- Shorter length of stay, better results, and high patient satisfaction rates.

What Can Be Revealed Through Data Analysis? The following scenarios are examples of deviations from the local norm that may become evident through data analysis:

- A practitioner with no documented evidence of participation in CME programs has a number of cases in which his or her management deviated from the accepted norm (as judged by the medical staff through its performance improvement process);
- The pathology tissue review process reveals that a practitioner has removed normal appendices at twice the local and national rates; and
- The transfusion-monitoring process notes that one practitioner orders blood transfused into a patient whose hemoglobin level is between 9.0 and 10.0, whereas the individual's peer group does so for a patient's whose hemoglobin level is 8.0.

If the goal of the reappraisal process is to identify good performance along with areas of needed improvement, these scenarios may present an opportunity for discussion between the chairperson and the practitioner. Factual data presented in a spirit of mutual respect often will effect the desired change in practice patterns.

A Need for Monitoring. Concerns identified through data analysis sometimes necessitate further investigation. Occasionally, a chairperson will note a trend toward the same undesirable performance throughout a department or a segment of the department's practitioners. The concern identified may be unrelated to a practitioner's performance and may be, instead, a systemic issue that requires attention from the hospital's management team. In such a case, a broad educational effort coupled with focused follow-up monitoring may be called for.

Other Information Data Analysis Can Uncover. The reasons for deviations sometimes may be evident in the data. For example, an obstetrician may have a patient population for whom the rate of Caesarean section deliveries is higher than the norm, or whose hospitalization is longer than the average length of stay. Further analysis may reveal that the practitioner also has a higher rate of indigent patients than the norm. These data might indicate a higher risk population due to lack of adequate prenatal care.

Unresolved Questions. Sometimes the data presented raise questions that remain unresolved. In these instances, further evaluation—either retrospective or concurrent—may be necessary. In situations in which the expiration of an applicant's previous appointment period is imminent, individuals who are evaluating the applicant's information may feel a sense of urgency and may believe that an all or nothing decision must be made. Several options are available under this circumstance, including

- Reappointment with the renewal of all clinical privileges and with the stipulation that further evaluation/monitoring (retrospective or concurrent) be conducted in the area of concern (for example, behavior, health, clinical performance) may be recommended;
- Reappointment and/or renewal of clinical privileges for a specified limited time, such as three or six months, to allow for further evaluation and resolution of the questions may be recommended, an option that may be reportable to the NPDB;
- Reappointment, renewal, or revision of most privileges, with the stipulation that monitoring or additional review requirements be placed on the procedures or diagnoses that remain in question, may be suggested; or

- A recommendation that includes continuing mandatory proctoring (concurrent or retrospective) may be made.

As long as there is no recommendation for denial or limitation of membership or clinical privileges, applicants need not be afforded the right to a hearing (unless the organization's bylaws, rules and regulations, or policies and procedures provide this right to the individual).

Use of an External Evaluator. There are times during the reappraisal, reappointment, and renewal of clinical privileges process when the available information is insufficient to make a decision or when prevailing circumstances make the decision less than impartial. This might occur, for example, in situations involving partnerships, friendships, competition issues, a small number of staff members for comparison of practice patterns, or a low volume or limited performance of a privilege within the organization. The chairperson may strive for fairness to the practitioner by choosing to seek an external evaluation through the use of a peer review consultant. Qualified individuals may be identified by referrals from professional associations (for example, American College of Surgeons, American College of Obstetricians and Gynecologists). Often, practitioners who are known to the medical staff and respected for their ability to perform or consult in a particular specialty are selected from nearby tertiary or academic institutions. The chairperson may also wish to seek data from another hospital where the LIP practices.

The accepted goal of the process should be to identify avenues for improvement rather than to limit an individual's ability to practice. If this goal is the underlying theme throughout the process, practitioners may be more accepting of the outcome.

Department Director and Executive Committee Recommendations

Department or major clinical service recommendations are an important piece of information used when making decisions on continued membership on the medical staff and in delineating individual clinical privileges. The applicant-specific statement or recommendation is often referred to as a substantive comment about the practitioner. If the department chairperson is a member of the same discipline with essentially equal qualifications, the recommendation may also serve as a peer recommendation. The department chairperson's recommendation is based on the LIP's evidence of licensure, current competence, and ability to perform, along with evidence of satisfactory performance in relation to the privileges requested. The chairperson's evaluations and recommendations are made after reviewing the application and the applicant's performance data described elsewhere in this chapter.

The department chair or chief of service must evaluate the individual's ability to perform the privileges requested. In instances in which there is doubt about an applicant's ability to perform the privileges requested, the medical executive committee may request an evaluation by someone other than the applicant's department chairperson or chief of service.

The Decision-making Process

The medical staff executive committee recommends individuals for medical staff membership and delineated clinical privileges. This applies to the initial appointment as well as to reappointment. These recommendations are forwarded to the governing body, which has the ultimate authority for these decisions.

With the recommendation for reappointment or renewal of clinical privileges from the department or section head (if applicable), the credentials and medical executive committee focuses on the problem areas identified by the department chair. In non-departmentalized hospitals, however, the first level of review may be the medical executive committee. In either case, the resultant findings and recommendations are documented and forwarded to the governing body.

The governing body is the final authority and reappoints the individual or renews, revises, or revokes the privileges requested. All privileges granted are fully delineated. For cases in which the governing body does not agree with the medical staff recommendation, bylaws or policies may require a review of the decision through a designated mechanism, such as the joint conference committee, or a reconsideration by a medical staff committee. The applicants then are notified of the outcome and advised of their right of appeal in accordance with the provisions in the medical staff bylaws. Each individual who has membership or clinical privileges is entitled to appeal an adverse outcome. Adverse outcomes that are upheld after the appeal process has been concluded or waived (for example, loss of membership, limitation/restriction/revocation of privileges) are reported to the NPDB through the state licensing agency.

Example 5-4, page 146, a reappointment and renewal of privileges form for Memorial Hospital, Fremont, Ohio, is a sample form signed by the chief of staff, department chairperson, credentials committee, medical executive committee, and board of trustees that formally approves an applicant's request for reappointment and renewal of clinical privileges.

Continuing Competence Assessment Through Continuous Reappraisal

If an identified deviation in practice leads to the conclusion that revision or revocation of privileges is necessary, it should be instituted immediately. Recommendations for additional education or the limitation of privileges should not await the periodic reappraisal, reappointment, and renewal of privileges process. This strategy is often referred to as continuous reappraisal. Continuous reappraisal

cannot replace the formal reappraisal, reappointment, and renewal of privileges process required by the Joint Commission, which documents the review and evaluation of an individual's performance and outcome throughout a specified one- to two-year period.

What Surveyors Look For

The Joint Commission evaluates the hospital's competence assessment process through the review of policies, procedures, and plans that are verified through interviews, observation, and a review of documents and records. Continuing competence assessment is achieved through many activities performed during the survey, including medical staff leadership interviews, review of credentials and privileging records, and on-site visits. This section covers only those items that surveyors will look for in assessing a hospital's continuing competence assessment process for LIPs covered by the Medical Staff standards.

During the medical staff credentials interview with the director of the medical staff and medical staff itself, the surveyor reviews credentials files of selected members of the medical staff and other individuals whose patient care activities are defined by the medical staff privileging process. The surveyor may ask those present to describe the process and the criteria for reappointing and renewing or revising clinical privileges.

During the medical staff leadership interview, the physician surveyor meets with the president of the medical staff, medical director, medical staff coordinator, chairpersons or section chiefs of medical staff departments, elected and appointed leaders of medical staff, and others. Suggested questions related to continuing competence assessment include

- How do medical staff leaders actively participate in processes to improve and maintain performance?

- What medical education activities does the hospital sponsor?
- How is the medical staff involved in leadership concerning measurement, assessment, and improvement in the following processes: medical assessment and treatment of patients; medication use; use of blood and blood components; use of operative and other procedures; efficiency of clinical practice patterns; and significant departures from established patterns of clinical practice?
- How does the hospital use assessment findings related to an individual's performance in the peer review process or in the continuing evaluations of LIPs'competence?

Common Problems in Assessing Continuing Competency for Licensed Independent Practitioners

Privileges or appointments cannot be granted to LIPs for a period of more than two years. Many hospitals struggle to complete the re-credentialing, re-privileging, and reappointment process within the two-year time frame. Extending initial appointments or clinical privileges is not allowed. Because of this time constraint, hospitals can find themselves in noncompliance with JCAHO's standards pertaining to timeliness in assessing continuing competency.

Improvement Tips for Assessing Continuing Competency

Improvement tips for hospitals that find themselves unable to complete the reappointment and re-privileging process within the two-year time frame include the following:

- Start the re-credentialing process sooner. For example, send reappointment/re-privileging recommendations to the board for approval four to six months before the privileges and appointments expire. Consider starting the entire process two to three months earlier than usual.
- Provide the practitioner with a list of his or her clinical privileges, and request review and revisions. Supply the required completion date for updated information.
- Specifically request any modification of clinical privileges, accompanied by information demonstrating current clinical competence of the privileges requested.
- Consider using creative approaches to facilitate the receipt of timely paperwork from LIPs.
- Establish and consistently apply a policy that requires LIPs to submit a completed reappointment/re-privileging application before the two-year deadline expires. Identify the time frame required. If an LIP misses the deadline, he or she must reapply as a new applicant.

As front-line providers of direct care in hospitals, LIPs must be competent to perform the privileges that they have been granted to perform. To ensure the provision of high-quality, safe, and effective patient care, hospital leaders must ensure the regular assessment of practitioners' competence.

REFERENCE

1. Joint Commission on Accreditation of Healthcare Organizations: *Lexicon: Dictionary of Health Care Terms, Organizations, and Acronyms (2nd Edition).* Oakbrook Terrace, IL: JCAHO, 1998.

EXAMPLES

Example 5-1

Biennial Application for 2001-2003 Reappointment & Renewal of Clinical Privileges

SILVER CROSS HOSPITAL
Joliet, IL

BIENNIAL APPLICATION FOR
2001 - 2003 REAPPOINTMENT & RENEWAL OF CLINICAL PRIVILEGES
Due Date Friday, November 9, 2001

NAME (Please Print):____William Baylis, MD_____
INTERNET E-MAIL ADDRESS (If Applicable):_____

THE ATTACHED PROVIDER PROFILE REPRESENTS THE INFORMATION LISTED FOR YOU ON OUR COMPUTER DATA BASE. PLEASE REVIEW AND *MAKE ANY CORRECTIONS DIRECTLY ON THE FORM.*

ATTACHED YOU WILL ALSO FIND A COPY OF YOUR CURRENT PRIVILEGES AT SILVER CROSS HOSPITAL. IF YOU ARE REQUESTING AN ADDITION OR DELETION TO YOUR CURRENT PRIVILEGES, PLEASE *INDICATE SO ON THE ATTACHED FORM AND CHECK THE APPROPRIATE BOX BELOW.* ANY ADDITIONS <u>REQUIRE</u> SUPPORTING DOCUMENTATION e.g. COURSES TAKEN, NUMBER OF CASES PERFORMED, ETC. NO ADDITIONAL PRIVILEGES WILL BE CONSIDERED WITHOUT THIS DOCUMENTATION.

☐ I am requesting changes to my privileges. ☐ I am requesting reappointment with my current privileges.

****

LICENSURE\MEDICAL STAFF APPOINTMENT

During the past year and a half (2000-Present) has your license to practice medicine been limited, reprimanded, suspended, and revoked, voluntarily or involuntarily surrendered or is it currently being challenged? *IF YES, GIVE DETAILS ON A SEPARATE SHEET.* YES_____ NO_____

Has your DEA (Federal narcotic license) <u>ever</u> been suspended, reprimanded, revoked, voluntarily or involuntarily surrendered or is it currently being challenged? *IF YES, GIVE DETAILS ON A SEPARATE SHEET.* YES_____ NO_____

Has your medical staff appointment and/or clinical privileges ever been denied, reprimanded, revoked, suspended, reduced, not renewed, voluntarily or involuntarily surrendered at any health care facility during the past two and a half years (2000 - Present)? *IF YES, GIVE DETAILS ON A SEPARATE SHEET.* YES_____ NO_____

****

MALPRACTICE CLAIMS

Number of claims filed, settled or lost during the past year and a half (2000 - Present)? _____
PLEASE GIVE DETAILS ON A SEPARATE SHEET.

****

CURRENT HOSPITAL AFFILIATIONS
(Other than Silver Cross Hospital and Provena Saint Joseph)

Institution:_____ Status:_____

Institution:_____ Status:_____
*Note: If you are not very active at Silver, please attach a copy of your reappt. letter from your most active hospital.
****

ABILITY TO PERFORM PRIVILEGES REQUESTED

Do you have any physical or mental condition, or do you use any chemical substance, including alcohol, which in any way affects your ability to practice medicine and exercise the clinical privileges requested with reasonable skill and safety? YES_____ NO_____
If yes, please explain.

Do you speak a language other than English fluently? If yes, language _____
****

- SEE REVERSE -

(continued on next page)

SOURCE: Silver Cross Hospital, Joliet, IL. Used with permission.

Biennial Application for 2001-2003 Reappointment & Renewal of Clinical Privileges (continued)

SILVER CROSS HOSPITAL
Joliet, IL

BIENNIAL APPLICATION FOR REAPPOINTMENT & RENEWAL OF CLINICAL PRIVILEGES
Due Date Friday, November 9, 2001

I hereby apply for medical staff reappointment and clinical privileges as required by Silver Cross Hospital's Bylaws and Policy of its Medical Staff.

APPLICANT'S CONSENT AND RELEASE: I hereby authorize Silver Cross Hospital to consult with administrators and members of the medical staff of other hospitals or institutions with which I have been associated and with others, including past and present malpractice carriers, who may have information bearing on my professional competence, character and ethical qualifications. I consent to the inspection of all documents and data, including peer review records at other hospitals and other sources of available data, that may be material to any evaluation of my professional qualifications and competence to carry out the clinical privileges requested, my pattern of practice, as well as my physical and mental health status and moral and ethical qualifications for medical staff membership. I consent to the release of such information, including otherwise privileged or confidential information, to Silver Cross Hospital. I also agree to assist Silver Cross Hospital, if necessary, in obtaining any information which is requested for evaluation of my qualifications and competence.

In addition, I hereby make, constitute, and appoint any duly appointed agent of Silver Cross Hospital as my true and lawful attorney in fact for me in my name, place, stead, and on my behalf and for my use and benefit, for the purpose of requesting, reviewing, copying, signing for, or otherwise acting for investigative purposes with respect to documents and information in the possession of the person or entity to whom a request is presented.

I release Silver Cross Hospital, its agents, employees and Medical Staff members from liability, claims, causes of action, and disputes for all acts performed in connection with evaluating my application and my credentials, qualifications, and practices.

I further release from liability, claims, causes of action, and disputes any and all individuals and organizations who in good faith and without malice provide information to Silver Cross Hospital concerning my professional competence, medical practice patterns, ethics, character, and other qualifications for staff appointment and clinical privileges.

I consent to the release of such information, including otherwise privileged or confidential information, to Silver Cross Hospital.

I agree that a photo copy or faxed copy of this release form may be used in place of my original signature.

I understand that if Silver Cross Hospital identifies a substantive falsification or omission on this application that my reappointment will automatically be rejected and not processed further.

_____   _____
Signature   Date

Example 5-2

Request for Reappointment and Renewal of Clinical Privileges

715 S. Taft Avenue   MEMORIAL HOSPITAL   Telephone: 419-334-6624
Fremont, OH 43420   Fax: 419-334-6602
                                    2002-2003
                   REQUEST FOR REAPPOINTMENT AND RENEWAL OF CLINICAL PRIVILEGES

Personal Identification Data - Please correct printed information in the space below.

#[PHYSNAME], #[DEGREE]

Primary Office Address: #[OFC1_ADDRS], #[OFC1_CITY], #[OFC1_STATE] #[OFC1_ZIP]
Telephone: #[OFC1_TEL]
Fax: #[OFC1_FAX]

Secondary Office Address: #[OFC2_ADDRS], #[OFC2_CITY], #[OFC2_STATE] #[OFC2_ZIP]
Telephone: #[OFC2_TEL]
Fax: #[OFC2_FAX]

Home Address: #[HOME_ADDRS], #[HOME_CITY], #[HOME_STATE] #[HOME_ZIP]
Telephone: #[HOME_TEL]

Current Staff Category: #[STATUS]

Reappointment Request
I request reappointment to my current staff category: Yes_____   No_____
I request reappointment and change staff category to:_____
I do not wish to continue my staff membership:_____

American Board Certification - Please review and update board certification status and dates.

Specialty	Certified	Initial Certification Date	Recertification Date	Expiration Date
#[SPECIALTY1]	#[BOARD_CRT1]	#[BD1_INIT]	#[BD1_RECERT]	#[BD1_EXP]
#[SPECIALTY2]	#[BOARD_CRT2]	#[BD2_INIT]	#[BD2_RECERT]	#[BD2_EXP]
#[SPECIALTY3]	#[BOARD_CRT3]	#[BD3_INIT]	#[BD3_RECERT]	#[BD3_EXP]

Licensure/Certification - Listed below are the current state license(s) that you hold. Please list additional state licenses that are not identified.

State	License Number	State	License Number
#[STATE_LIC1]	#[LICENSE_NO]		
#[STATE_LIC2]	#[LICENSE_2]		
#[STATE_LIC3]	#[LICENSE_3]		
#[STATE_LIC4]	#[LICENSE_4]		

Do you maintain current certification in any of the following?   Expiration Date
ACLS (Advanced Cardiac Life Support)   Yes_____   No_____   #[ACLS_DATE]
ATLS (Advanced Trauma Life Support)   Yes_____   No_____   #[TRAUMA_EXP]
PALS (Pediatric Advanced Life Support)   Yes_____   No_____   #[PAL]
Neonatal Resuscitation   Yes_____   No_____   #[NEO_DATE]

Continuing Medical Education - Please provide continuing medical education courses and credits (meetings, pulications, etc.) for the past three years or attach listing.

_____
_____

Hospital Affiliations - Listed below are your current hospital affiliations on file in the Medical Staff Services Department at Memorial Hospital. Please provide names of institutions that are not listed.

Hospital	City	Hospital	City
#[HOSP_AFIL1]	#[CITY_AFIL1]		
#[HOSP_AFIL2]	#[CITY_AFIL2]		
#[HOSP_AFIL3]	#[CITY_AFIL3]		
#[HOSP_AFIL4]	#[CITY_AFIL4]		
#[HOSP_AFIL5]	#[CITY_AFIL5]		
#[HOSP_AFIL6]	#[CITY_AFIL6]		
#[HOSP_AFIL7]	#[CITY_AFIL7]		
#[HOSP_AFIL8]	#[CITY_AFIL8]		
#[HOSP_AFIL9]	#[CITY_AFIL9]		
#[HOSP_AFI10]	#[CITY_AFI10]		

(continued on next page)

EXAMPLES

Request for Reappointment and Renewal of Clinical Privileges (continued)

If the answer to any of the following questions is **YES**, please provide a full explanation of the details, and attach.

Since appointment or last reappointment to the Medical Staff:

Yes_____ No_____ Have any professional liability suits been filed against you?

Yes_____ No_____ Have any professional liability suits been filed against you which are presently pending?

Yes_____ No_____ Have any judgments or settlements been made against you in any professional liability cases?

Yes_____ No_____ Do you have a physical or mental condition which could affect your ability to exercise the clinical privileges requested or would require an accommodation in order for you to exercise the privileges requested safely and competently?

Yes_____ No_____ Are you currently engaged in the unlawful use of drugs?

Yes_____ No_____ Has your license to practice medicine, other professional licensure, or your DEA registration been terminated, limited, or suspended, either voluntarily or involuntarily?

Yes_____ No_____ Has your request for any specific clinical privileges changed?

Yes_____ No_____ Has the nature of your medical practice changed?

Yes_____ No_____ Have you been refused membership on any health care provider staff?

Yes_____ No_____ Has your membership status and/or clinical privileges on any health care provider staff been terminated, limited, or suspended, either voluntarily or involuntarily?

Yes_____ No_____ Has your membership in local, state or national professional societies or licensing bodies been terminated, limited, or suspended, either voluntarily or involuntarily?

APPLICANT'S CONSENT AND RELEASE

In making application for reappointment to the Medical Staff of Memorial Hospital I agree to abide by its Bylaws and by all Rules and Regulations. I hereby certify that the above statements are true to the best of my knowledge and that I am physically and mentally capable of performing the privileges for which I have applied. I pledge to provide for continuous care of my patients.

By applying for reappointment to the Medical Staff and for the exercise of specific clinical privileges, I hereby authorize the hospital, its Medical Staff and their representatives to consult with administrators and members of medical staffs of other hospitals or institutions with which I have been associated and with others, including past and present malpractice carriers, who may have information bearing on my professional competence, character and ethical qualifications.

I hereby further consent to the inspection by the hospital, its medical staff and their representatives of all records and documents, including medical records at other hospitals, that may be material to an evaluation of my professional qualifications and competence to carry out the clinical privileges requested as well as my moral and ethical qualifications for staff appointment.

I hereby release from liability all representatives of the hospital and its medical staff for their acts performed in good faith and without malice in connection with evaluating my application and my credentials and qualifications, and I hereby release from any liability any and all individuals and organizations who provide information to the hospital or its medical staff, in good faith and without malice, concerning my professional competence, ethics, character and other qualifications for staff appointment and clinical privileges, and I hereby consent to the release of such information.

I hereby further authorize and consent to the release by this hospital or its medical staff, to other hospitals or their medical staffs and to medical associations, of any information the hospital and medical staff may have concerning my professional competence, ethics, character and other professional qualifications, as long as such release of information is done in good faith and without malice, and I hereby release from liability this hospital and its medical staff for so doing.

I hereby further consent to exhaust all internal medical staff and hospital channels to resolve disputes before pursuing outside litigation on matters of quality assurance, peer review, quality of care issues and inter-personal relationships.

_____   _____   _____
Printed Name of Applicant   Signature of Applicant   Date
creden/r-applic.ms

(continued on next page)

Request for Reappointment and Renewal of Clinical Privileges (continued)

MEMORIAL HOSPITAL
Fremont, OH 43420

REQUEST FOR REAPPOINTMENT OF CLINICAL PRIVILEGES
2002-2003

TO: #[FIRSTNAME] #[LASTNAME], #[DEGREE]

FROM: Denise K. Woolley, CMSC, CPCS, Director, Medical Staff Services

DATE: August 1, 2001

SUBJECT: **Delineation of Privileges**

Attached you will find a copy of your current delineation of privileges. Please review each privilege/procedure that has been granted to you. Indicate below if you wish to continue your current privileges, or make any additions or deletions.

_____   I have reviewed the attached delineation of privilege form.
I *do not* wish to make any changes to my clinical privileges.

_____   I have reviewed the attached delineation of privilege form.
I wish to make the following additions and/or deletions:

_____
_____
_____
_____

Attach documentation of additional training and/or
experience to substantiate additional privileges requested.

_____   _____
Practitioner Signature   Date

EXAMPLES

Example 5-3

Samaritan Pacific Health Services General Hospital Policy on Peer Review

SAMARITAN PACIFIC HEALTH SERVICES, INC.

Newport, Oregon

GENERAL HOSPITAL POLICY

SUBJECT: **PEER REVIEW**				# 219.00				
Written: 1/89				Effective Date: 1/89				
Reviewed/Revised:	5/89	6/92	7/96	3/01				

I. POLICY

Samaritan Pacific Health Services, Inc. (SPHS) and the Samaritan Pacific Communities Hospital (SPCH) Medical Staff are responsible for the quality of care provided to its patient population. Therefore, it is the policy of SPHS to support the Medical Staff peer review process, a non-biased activity performed by the Medical Staff to measure, assess and, where necessary, improve performance on a hospital-wide basis. The peer review activities are completed at the direction of the Medical Staff Committees. **All Medical Staff peer review is privileged and confidential pursuant to ORS 41.675. All peer review case discussion must be within Executive Session of Medical Staff committees.**

For purposes of this policy, "physician" is intended to include all independent licensed practitioners (MD, DO, DPM, NP, CRNA, etc.) who have been granted Medical Staff membership and/or clinical privileges by the SPHS Board.

II. GENERAL REQUIREMENTS

A. The physician acted in good faith;
B. The physician acted in a manner reasonably believed to be in the best interests of SPHS; and
C. The physician acted without any reasonable cause to believe the conduct was unlawful.

III. PROCEDURE

A. Peer Review Program Components

The responsibility for peer review is delegated by the SPHS Board to the SPCH Medical Staff. The peer review process performed by the Medical Staff contains the following components:

1. Definitions of circumstances initiating the peer review process are listed below. This list may be revised by the Medical Staff committees, with approval by the SPHS Board. The process includes: 1) cases referred to a physician reviewer for an initial screening review; 2) cases referred to a Medical Staff committee by a physician reviewer; 3) cases referred by Medical Staff committees for Medical Executive Credentials Committee (MECC) review; and 4) cases referred by MECC for external review.

2. Generic circumstances or indicators for an initial screening include:

   a) Unpredictable deaths, deaths within 24 hours of hospital admission, postoperative death, patient suicide, and/or any other type of patient death defined through the medical staff committee process and approved for review.

   b) Unpredictable complications in patient condition and/or care or treatment, including those that result in major permanent loss of function, not related to the natural course of the patient's illness or underlying condition.

   c) Infant abduction or infant discharge to the wrong family

   d) Rape (by another patient or staff)

   e) Surgery on the wrong patient or wrong body part.

   f) Predictable complications.

   g) Postoperative complications or an unexpected return to surgery.

#219.00 Peer Review

(continued on next page)

Samaritan Pacific Health Services General Hospital Policy on Peer Review
(continued)

    h)   Readmission within 14 days of discharge.

    i)   Moderate to severe adverse drug reactions.

    j)   All blood product transfusions.

    l)   Trends of patient and/or staff complaints involving a physician.

    m) Utilization issues or concerns.

    n)   Patient leaving against medical advice (AMA).

    o)   Minor patient on SCF hold.

    p)   OMPRO review requests.

3. Specific circumstances for an initial screening may include:

    a)   Lack of timeliness, completeness, accuracy, legibility of Medical Records.

    b)   Lack of responsiveness to hospital and/or Medical Staff committee requests.

    c)   Referrals from parties such as Nurse Managers or Administration through the QM/RM Director or Medical Staff committee Chair.

    d)   Other service-specific defined performance indicators, as established and approved by the Medical Staff committee and approved by the MECC.

4. Peer Review Process Participants:

    a)   For the purposes of the peer review program, a peer reviewer is defined as an Active status member of the Medical Staff, in good standing, with privileges in the same medical specialty or a related medical specialty. The Peer Review Panel and External Review provide for non-MD/DO participation.

    b)   Every reasonable attempt will be made to ensure that the peer reviewer is impartial and unbiased toward the physician whose case is under review.

    c)   A peer reviewer will not have participated, either formally or informally, in the case under review. However, *opinions* and *information* may be obtained from physicians who were involved in the case.

5. Selection of Peer Review Panels for Special Circumstances:

    Peer review panels may be selected by the MECC when additional expertise would benefit the review of a case. Panelists may be selected for their expertise in a given area of medicine or in a specific medical specialty. A peer review panel may be utilized when a non-MD/DO has a case under review. All members of a peer review panel need not be Active status Medical Staff members.

6. Peer Review Activity Time Frames:

    a)   Cases referred to Medical Staff committees for peer review are to be reviewed in a timely manner, and generally at the next regularly scheduled meeting.

    b)   Cases are identified for peer review through an ongoing retrospective record review upon completion of medical record coding and record completion.

    c)   Cases are identified for peer review on a concurrent basis during routine quality and utilization review activities. Those cases requiring immediate review, will be referred to the appropriate Medical Staff committee Chair. Cases determined to require immediate Medical Staff committee review by the Chair will be referred to the committee at their next meeting. Cases determined not to require immediate review will undergo the medical record completion process prior to referral to committee.

2

(continued on next page)

Samaritan Pacific Health Services General Hospital Policy on Peer Review (continued)

7. Circumstances that may initiate external peer review include the following:

   a) The Medical Staff committee cannot make a determination without additional information from a physician with specialized expertise.

   b) The physician whose case is under review requests external peer review by submitting a written statement detailing the reason for the request.

   c) The MECC requests external review.

8. An unbiased physician in the applicable specialty will be asked to perform the external review. External review may also be appropriate when the physician whose case is under review is the sole specialist on the Medical Staff, or all other appropriate peer reviewers are either partners or in direct financial competition.

9. Participation in the peer review process by the physician whose case is under review.

   A case may be referred to a Medical Staff committee by the initial screening physician reviewer. If the Medical Staff committee has concerns/questions about the case after its initial review, it may either communicate with the physician whose case is under review in writing, or invite the physician to attend the next Medical Staff committee meeting. When the Medical Staff committee review is complete, and if their recommendation is either a marginal or significant deviation from the standard of care, the case is automatically referred to the MECC.

   The MECC will notify the physician whose case is under review that the Medical Staff committee found either a Marginal or Significant Deviation from the Standard of Care and provide the physician an opportunity to address the MECC at the meeting where the case is being reviewed, or to provide a written statement to the MECC in advance of the meeting date.

B. **Peer Review Program Methodology**

1. The peer review program is consistent — all cases referred for peer review shall follow the peer review program components listed above.

2. All efforts will be made to complete the peer review process as soon as practicable.

3. Conclusions of review are defensible. All cases undergoing peer review will have a peer review form completed that lists the rationale for the conclusion made by the peer reviewer(s). Rationale must be based on the reason the case was reviewed, and supported by current clinical practice, practice guidelines and/or literature.

4. Peer review is balanced. All opinions regarding medical management, including minority opinions, of the case under review will be considered in the ultimate determination of the case. This includes information and opinions from the individual whose case is under review.

5. Results of peer review are evaluated at the time of a physician's application for Medical Staff reappointment and are utilized to improve the hospital's performance in individual situations, and, as a whole:

   a) Results of peer review activities are aggregated and reported at the time of Medical Staff reappointment to evaluate a physician's competency and/or request for clinical privileges. A physician specific performance profile is completed and reviewed by the Medical Staff Service Committee Chair and MECC prior to recommending a physician's reappointment.

   b) Results of peer review activities are utilized in the hospital-wide performance improvement program to facilitate organizational improvement.

6. Conclusions, outcomes and actions resulting from peer review are monitored for effectiveness.

3

(continued on next page)

Samaritan Pacific Health Services General Hospital Policy on Peer Review (continued)

7. Information relating to peer review activities of Medical Staff committees may be made available in Executive Session of a Medical Staff committee to:
   a) Physician whose case is under review shall receive only information concerning the aspects of his/her practice which are under consideration;
   b) Physician Medical Staff committee members;
   c) The Administrator or his/her designee;
   d) The Director of Clinical Services;
   e) The Quality/Risk Management Director;
   f) The Medical Staff Coordinator; and
   g) The Chief of Staff, Members of the MECC, and Board of Directors

8. The Medical Staff Coordinator will maintain a permanent and secure file of Medical Staff committee peer review documents and correspondence. Access to these files outside of Medical Staff committee meetings shall be limited to the individuals listed above during normal working hours. Access shall be given only in the presence of the Medical Staff Coordinator or the QM/RM Director. At no time are copies of peer review materials given to anyone external to the peer review process as defined above. This includes the physician whose case is under review. All discussion relating to peer review cases must be within the Executive Session of the Medical Staff committees.

9. All provisions for confidentiality and access to Medical Staff committee peer review materials shall also apply to physician credentialing and peer review files. A physician may authorize release of information, if originally provided by the physician, from his/her own credentials file by written consent to the Medical Staff Coordinator or Administrator. Physician credentialing and peer review documents obtained from a source other than the physician are protected under ORS 41.675 and will not be copied or released.

10. Notwithstanding the above, SPCH will comply with any legal order from a court of law or other legal requirements to release this information.

11. Violations of this policy and confidentiality violations regarding peer review shall be reported to the MECC and/or the Administrator for appropriate action.

12. The flow of information in the peer review process is represented in the first attachment.

13. Subsequent attachments are examples of documents which may initiate or relate to peer review:

    ORS 41.675 – Peer Review Statute
    Peer Review Form
    Peer Review Outcome/Action Codes
    Medical Records Rating Form
    Blood Utilization Review Form
    Confidential Occurrence Report Form
    Complaint Form
    Practitioner Detail & Summary Peer Reviews with service aggregate data

    *This revised policy replaces Policy #224.50 "External Peer Review" and
    Policy #220 "Confidentiality of Medical Staff Credentialing and Peer Review Information".*

Reviewed and Recommended:

_____   Date: _____
Chief of Staff

_____   Date: _____
Administrator

OB/Peds 3-6-01
Medicine Service 3-7-01
Medical Practices 3-8-01
Surgery Service 3-12-01
MECC/Administrator 3-21-01
PCHD Board 3-29-01
Medical Staff for Information 3-28-01

4

EXAMPLES

Example 5-4

Reappointment and Renewal of Clinical Privileges

Memorial Hospital   Fremont, OH 43420

Reappointment and Renewal of Clinical Privileges
2002-2003

#[FIRSTNAME] #[LASTNAME], #[DEGREE]

I have reviewed the above referenced practitioner's Request for Reappointment and Renewal of Clinical Privileges application, Request for Reappointment of Clinical Privileges, and Profile for Reappointment to the Medical Staff.

There is documentation in the practitioner's reappointment credentials file that indicates that all Medical Staff approved standards for reappointment and privileges have been fulfilled. My review and evaluation is based upon all quality improvement monitoring functions, performance of clinical judgment and technical skills, physical and emotional health, and personal/professional peer relationships. I recommend reappointment to the Medical Staff and that the requested clinical privileges be approved.

_____No exception
_____Exceptions, specify with reason_____

_____

Comments_____

_____
Signature: **Service Chief**   Date

_____No exception
_____Exceptions, specify with reason_____

_____

Comments_____

_____
Signature: **Department Chairman**   Date

* * * * *

Credentials Committee concurred with the Service Chief and Department Chairman:_____
                                                                          Date
Comments_____

* * * * *

Medical Executive Committee concurred with the Credentials Committee:_____
                                                                          Date
Comments_____

* * * * *

Board of Trustees concurred with the Medical Executive Committee:_____
                                                                          Date
Comments_____

SOURCE: Memorial Hospital, Fremont, OH. Used with permission

Selected Readings

Berger JT: Culture and ethnicity in clinical care. *Arch Intern Med* 158:2085–2095, 1998.

Boylan CR, Westra R: Meeting Joint Commission requirements for staff nurse competency. *J Nurs Care Qual* 12(4): 44–48, Apr 1998.

Britton BP, Raper JT, Walden CM: From development to evaluation: Making a competency plan work. *J Nurs Staff Dev* 11(4): 210–214, Jul/Aug 1995.

Brushing up on competence assessment. *Joint Commission Perspectives* 21(1): 6–7, Jan 2001.

Burke A: How to accomplish organization-wide competency and education. *Nurs Manage* 31(2): 30–26, Feb 2000.

Chard RR: Using a case scenario approach to evaluate age-specific competencies. *AORN Journ* 67(3): 634–642, Mar 1998.

Claflin N: A practical approach to competence assessment. *J for Healthcare Quality* 19(6): 12–18.

Competency assessment begins at orientation. *Same-Day Surgery* Apr 2000, pp. 44–45.

Darr K: Credentialing: The special problem of *locum tenens* physicians. *Hospital Topics,* Sept-Nov 2001.

Decker PJ: The hidden competencies of healthcare: Why self-esteem, accountability, and professionalism may affect hospital customer satisfaction scores. *Hospital Topics* 77(1): 14–26, Winter 1999.

Decker PJ, Strader MK, and Wise RJ: Beyond JCAHO: Using competency models to improve healthcare organizations, Part 1. *Hosp Topics* 75(1): 23–28, Winter 1997.

Decker PJ, Strader MK, and Wise RJ: Beyond JCAHO: Using competency models to improve healthcare organizations, Part 2: Developing competence assessment systems. *Hosp Topics* 75(2): 10–17, Spring 1997.

Esque TJ, Gilbert TF: Making competencies pay off. *Training* Jan 1995, pp. 16–19.

Huffman M: Competency-based orientation for perioperative cardiovascular nurses. *AORN Journal* 61(4): 722–729, Apr 1995.

Joint Commission: *Credentials Review and Privileging: Questions and Answers for Ambulatory*

Care. Oakbrook Terrace, IL: Joint Commission on Accreditation of Healthcare Organizations, 1999.

Joint Commission: *Credentials Review, Clinical Responsibilities, and Competence Assessment: Questions and Answers for Behavioral Health Care Organizations.* Oakbrook Terrace, IL: Joint Commission on Accreditation of Healthcare Organizations, 1999.

Joint Commission: *Joint Commission Guide to Allied Health Professionals.* Oakbrook Terrace, IL: Joint Commission on Accreditation of Healthcare Organizations, 2002.

Joint Commission: *The Medical Staff Handbook: A Guide to Joint Commission Standards.* Oakbrook Terrace, IL: Joint Commission on Accreditation of Healthcare Organizations, 1999.

Kelly-Thomas KJ: *Clinical and Nursing Staff Development: Current Competence, Future Focus.* Philadelphia: Lippincott Williams and Wilkins, 1998.

Marshall JM, Adams JP, Janich JA: Practical, continuing competency-assessment program for pharmacists and technicians. *Am J Health-Syst Pharm* 54:1412–1417, Jun 15, 1997.

Martin AE, Stumpf JL, Ryan ML: Assessing pharmacists' competence in clinical information retrieval. *Am J Health-Syst Pharm* 53:2957–2958, Dec 15, 1996.

McConnell EA: Competence vs. competency. *Nurs Manage* 32(5): 14, May 2001.

McLagan PA: Competencies: The next generation. *Training & Development* May 1997, pp. 40–47.

National Institutes of Health Office of Human Resources Management, Clinical Center Education & Training: Competency. <*http://ohrm.cc.nih.gov/ train/competency/corecomp.html*> (accessed Jan 14, 2002).

O'Grady T, O'Brien A: A guide to competency-based orientation. *J Nurs Staff Development,* May/June 1992, pp. 128–133.

Parsons EC, Capka MB: Building a successful risk-based competency assessment model. *AORN J* 66(6): 1065–1071, Dec 1997.

Robbins CJ, et al: Developing leadership in health-care administration: A competency assessment tool/Practitioner application. *J of Healthcare Manage* 46(3): 188–202, May/Jun 2001.

Robinson SM, Barberis-Ryan C: Competency assessment: A systematic approach. *Nurs Manage* 26(2): 40–44, Feb 1995.

Shaffer F, Kobs A: Measuring competencies of temporary staff. *Nurs Manage* 28(5): 41–42, 44–45, May 1997.

Spencer LM, and Spencer SM: *Competence at Work.* New York: John Wiley & Sons, 1993.

Thompson RE: Recredentialing: Reappointment and renewal of clinical privileges. *Synergy* 25(2): 24–25, 28, Feb 1998.

Umiker W: The challenge of competency assessment. *Health Care Supervisor* 17(3): 11–17, Mar 1999.

Watson RL, Gorbunoff E, Boyce DM: A clinical competency program for nurses caring for infants and children receiving conscious sedation. *J Emerg Nurs* 24(1): 85–9, Feb 1998.

Wick JY, Zanni GR: Cultural competence: A pragmatic plan for fulfilling a professional imperative. *The Consultant Pharmacist* 16(3): 197–211, Mar 2001.

Index